MAGIC EYES ■■■■■■■■■■■■■■■■■■■■■■■■■■■■■■■■■

■■■MAGIC EYES

SCENES FROM AN ANDEAN GIRLHOOD ■■■■■■■■■■■■■■■■

■■■■■■■■■■■■■■■■■■■■■■■■■■ BY WENDY EWALD ■■■■■■■■■

FROM STORIES TOLD BY ALICIA AND MARÍA VÁSQUEZ ■■■■

■■■■■■■■■■■■■■■■■■■■■■■■■■■■■■■■ PHOTOGRAPHS BY

WENDY EWALD AND CHILDREN OF RÁQUIRA, COLOMBIA ■■■

■■■■■■■■■■■■■■■■■■■■■■■ BAY PRESS, SEATTLE ■1992

Bay Press
115 West Denny Way, Seattle, WA 98119

Magic Eyes
was produced by Katy Homans and Nan Richardson/Umbra Editions, Inc., New York;
designed by Katy Homans and edited by Nan Richardson.
The stories were first edited by Tom McDonough.
The separations and printing are by Becotte and Gershwin, Horsham, PA
The paper is Mohawk Vellum 100# cream white.

Library of Congress Cataloging-in-Publication Data
Ewald, Wendy.
Magic Eyes: scenes from and Andean girlhood/by Wendy Ewald;
from stories told by Alicia and María Vásquez; photographs by Wendy Ewald
and the children of Ráquira, Colombia.
p. cm.
s-ck—
ISBN 0-941920-21-6 (pbk.)
1. Ráquira (Colombia)—Social conditions. 2. Ráquira (Colombia)—Social conditions—Pictorial
works. 3. Vásquez, Alicia. 4. Rural women—Colombia—Ráquira—Biography.
5. Children—Colombia—Ráquira—Social conditions. I. Title.
HN310.R37E9 1992   92-53269
                                                                                                            CIP
Printed in the United States of America
First Printing 1992

The names of the Vásquez family members, as well as certain details of events and places,
have been changed in the interest of privacy and political safety.
Additionally, some characters described in the chapter
"Blind Ana Comes to Visit" were drawn from outside the Valley region.

Acknowledgments

I have had help from many people along the way in the making of this book but none more than from my husband, Tom McDonough, who helped me transform hundreds of pages of transcripts into a literate story. His belief in the project and sense of language guided me at all times.

I am grateful to Katy Homans and Nan Richardson for the energy they put into finding a home for the book, for their help in weaving together the words and the pictures, and to Katy for her remarkable design. I want to thank Ted Rosengarten, Scott Spencer, Ariel Dorfman, Kathleen Ross, Ben Lifson, Iris Hill, Alma Guillermoprieto and especially Chuck Verrill for reading the manuscript and offering their suggestions. The Lyndhurst Foundation, the Fulbright Commission, the Kentucky Foundation for Women, the Polaroid Foundation and the New York Foundation for the Arts provided financial support for the project and long birth of the book. My parents Ted and Carolyn Ewald and sister Holly Ewald gave me emotional support, as did Robert Coles, who continued to have faith in me.

In Colombia, there are many people without whose help I could not have carried on my work: Ezequiel Alarcón and John Orbell, who worked with me and the children in Ráquira, Patricia Conway, who introduced me to Alicia and kept us in touch, Bernardo Gutierrez, Leonel Girardo, Adelaida Trujillo and Carlos Mejía who provided warmth and humour, and finally the Vásquez family, without whose strength, compassion and sense of duty this book wouldn't be possible — especially Alicia, who believed that her story could help others.

— W. E.

For Alicia, who suggested that I begin this book, and for Tom, who insisted that I finish it, with love

How the Story was Made

In 1982 I settled in Ráquira, a small village of potters in a cool desert valley on the western spine of the Colombian Andes. For nearly two years I photographed there and in other parts of Colombia while teaching in a tiny village classroom. My fifth graders were the oldest students in the primary school, ranging from nine to sixteen years old, in their final year of education. Most of them lived in the mountains above the town and rose before dawn to tend the crops and cattle that would occupy them for the rest of their lives. I shared what might be called the last year of their childhood.

The children learned to shoot, develop, and print their own photographs. I lent them Polaroid and Instamatic cameras and gave them assignments to photograph and write about themselves, their families, their animals, and their fantasies.

At first they had difficulties with the camera. Instead of framing someone's face, as they intended, they often photographed his knees or feet. There were no windows in the mountain huts where they slept, and they had rarely seen television, so the idea of "framing" was utterly foreign to them: they had never seen their surroundings *through* anything. I asked them to carry a piece of paper with a hole in it and look through it at everything they came upon. Within a couple of weeks the problem of using the viewfinder was solved.

My students brought their exposed film to school and developed it in the little darkroom I built in a room of a colonial house in the village. During all these months they never damaged a roll of film; few experienced photographers could say the same. Being careful came naturally to the children. They had been making pots since they were five years old.

Towards the end of my project in Ráquira, I met Alicia. We were introduced by a mutual friend who was helping her rebuild her house. She lived in barrio Luis Alberto Vega, a squatter settlement constructed on land claimed from one of the steep slopes of the Andes which bound Bogotá on the east and west. Alicia was then twenty-eight, a single mother of three young boys, who ran a craft cooperative for the women in her barrio and a milk program for the children. She had a quiet self-assurance and authority as she began to speak of her life, past and present.

In Ráquira I had become fascinated with the rugged world of the Colombian countryside, deeply rooted in magic. Alicia read one of the interviews recorded with my students — an account of a shepherd girl accused by the villagers of being a witch. "This is just like my life," she said. "Can you help me write my story down?" Although Alicia's family had come to the city when she was a child, her deepest ties were with a universe that had much in common with that of my students.

Over time we exchanged stories and later books. One day I picked out Balzac's *In Search of the Absolute,* from a box of books left by a journalist friend. Alicia buried it in her grocery basket, and said she would look at it that night, when the children went to bed.

Two days later, over coffee in her tarpaper house, Alicia recited Balzac's story. She had read it by candlelight and then told the story to her children. She asked if I could please bring more books. The novels soon became as real to Alicia's family as soap operas.

"This isn't just fiction," she said. "It can't be. Because if it were only fiction these characters could not touch you so deeply. When I read a book, I feel what the characters feel, and when I've finished reading it, I'm completely convinced that I've read real things."

The day she finished García Márquez's *One Hundred Years of Solitude,* we climbed for hours in the mountains of her childhood. Recounting the saga of the Buendías, Alicia explained how it related to her family: the pig's tail that the cursed Buendías were born with was similar, she said, to the evil eye her family was cursed with.

I told her that I had read that the ancient Syrians believed the world was created by a pair of eyes — the gaze of God himself. This belief spread with the Arab invasion of India, through the Mediterranean, Africa, and the Iberian peninsula, until the Spanish exported it to South America. Each culture changed the concept and gave it its own form and meaning.

In the case of Alicia's family, *mal de ojo,* the evil eye, was a curse that had its origin in the confrontation between the Indians and the Spanish at the time of the conquest. The blue-eyed, light-skinned Spanish usurped the Indians' land with the magical power of their horses and guns. Though Spain is present-day Colombia's principal cultural model, among its deeply Indian population a suspicion of people with light hair, light skin and especially, blue eyes remains. If a family prospers and attracts the attention of someone with this power, bad luck and misfortune may follow.

To protect themselves, people darken their eyelids; mascara originated as a charm against the evil eye. In Colombia these charms are called *contras.* Children still wear *contras* such as beads, plastic horns, or nutmeg to protect themselves. The evil eye is not a power which is desired, nor can it be controlled.

Growing up, Alicia tried to use her power to confront the impossible situations she was in and to break out of her poverty. As an adult she understood that she must use it to fight against the powers she saw lined up against her — the Catholic church and the government which kept her family and one million people in Bogotá homeless.

Alicia told me her stories by candlelight after she'd put her children to sleep, drawing me in with her often extreme perception and sensitivity. Her storytelling became more and more detailed as she relived her childhood. She shook, cried and sweated. Sometimes she even acted the part of young Alicia. Later she told me these sessions had somehow freed her from the fright and self-loathing of her childhood — as if a weight had been lifted.

Alicia's stories referred often to her mother. She admired María, but sometimes blamed their relationship for her difficult childhood. A thin, handsome woman with dark skin and Indian features, María came to cook lunch for Alicia's children one day while Alicia delivered the lamps and tapestries the cooperative had made. María offered to add to the Vásquez history — describing the home she'd left behind in El Valle and the struggle she faced as a single mother in Bogotá. She came to tea in my apartment overlooking the city and told me stories from the coffee farms of her childhood: stories of witches, curses, and buried treasure.

As I became more involved with the Vásquez women, it seemed important to narrate visually the stories of Alicia and others in her family, but the camera made Alicia uncomfortable. She dreamed of a lens pursuing her — like the evil eye. I decided instead to concentrate on photographing the Vásquez' neighbors and countrymen living in similar circumstances.

The stories of the Vásquez family are true. For me, they were a way of understanding recent Colombian history, as well as grasping the significance of the peasant movement from the country to the city, a tidal change throughout Latin America today. Marco Tulio, Alicia's grandfather, had immigrated with thousands of others from the province of Antioquia, which I learned was now home to the *narco-traficantes*. The invasion of the barrio Policarpa Salavarrieta, one of the first and most publicized takeovers of private land by homeless families, was the beginning of an important political and social movement in Colombian cities, which continued in the 1980s. The 1977 general strike, which Alicia participated in, provided the excuse the military needed to intervene in the government: in the next few years sixty thousand people were arrested to combat "subversion." In 1977, before Javier Vásquez's enlistment in the army, the brother of the defense minister was found with cocaine on a military plane.

"Life is hard," Alicia said one night. "Things change. The way you think changes. But along the way there are strange things that come to you . . . you can't imagine. Even if I have nothing, I've got to feel I'm worth something. An easy life doesn't teach you how to live."

She held up a paper negative printed on a postcard — the only picture she had of herself as a little girl. "No one ever listened to me or looked at me before," she said, offering it.

It had been taken by an itinerant photographer in the small quiet square by the Gold Museum near the bustling corner where the emerald dealers trade. For thirty years this photographer had been making pictures by removing the lens cap — formerly the top of a rum bottle — and quickly replacing it. He had posed Alicia's mother, María, along with Alicia, her brother Javier, a neighbor woman and the neighbor's daughter — all in front of a '44 Lincoln, as if the car belonged to them.

The photographer's technique, typical of street portraitists in Colombia, was to make a paper negative in his portable darkroom, which consisted of two tiny trays of chemicals inside the camera itself. He mounted the negative on a hook in front of the camera and photographed it, producing a positive image. His clients, if they wanted to keep the negative, got two pictures for the price of one. Alicia had kept the negative. To compensate for the black faces on the negative image, she tinted the faces with a pink magic marker. The crude coloring made the faces pop out, like the faces of ghosts.

"All I'm trying to do," Alicia kept repeating, "is tell you about my life the best way I can."

This book is a collaboration of voices. The children of Ráquira taught me about their own history, the rhythms of rural life, about a countryside marked by magic, suffering, passion and religion. Their images glimpse a different world, sometimes secretive. It was Alicia who first offered me the gift of real contact and understanding of that world. Because she had left the countryside as a girl, she was no longer under the spell of her peasant past: she could order it and explain it. She was the teacher, and I the student: her words, spoken and remembered, retold, recorded, transcribed and then rewritten, form a continuous portrait of a place: unposed, yet formalized in the making of this book. That process of transcription and editing defines a space, the gaps between the known and still unknown: the mystery of some common destiny that Alicia, the children, and I all share (though our circumstances are different) with the reader of this book.

This story begins with the trip we took together to Pan de Azúcar, the village of Alicia's childhood, in search of her father's fate — which she feared might be her own.

— WENDY EWALD, RHINEBECK, NY 1992

Mama says that when I was born my eyes were blue-green. They were divine, they were stars — sharp-edged instead of round. They sparkled and jumped out at you. Mama's eyes were fierce. ■ I liked to look at Papa's eyes; they were light.

In the mountains, you live what you see, you see what you live. In the valley, where Grandfather built his house, under the wide-open, gentle mountains, everything looked tiny: the houses looked like those little huts we made with mud after it rained; and the livestock and cane fields looked like toys. At dusk, when the sky behind the stone fences was dark, and sun shone through the gaps where the stones touch, the fences looked like lace sewn to the slope of the mountains. Sometimes the dunes across the valley looked like the dinosaurs we'd seen in the illustrated encyclopedia Grandfather Leónidas had, with their skin all pitted by cow paths, and the fences were the scales ridging their backs. Grandfather had more coffee trees than anyone else. At harvest time, they spread the coffee berries on the ground in front of the house. My job was to rake them with a rake that was taller than me. ■ It was late afternoon and the breeze was beginning to blow cool. Papa was crossing the valley with his burro loaded up with coffee sacks. I watched him disappearing and appearing in and out of the banana trees. ■ He called my name. I ran to the hill. He slapped the donkey towards the house and waved at me. ■ "Come on, baby. Let me hold you." He lifted me up so my face was next to his, and he smiled. I said, "Papa," and tugged at his cape. He began to stare at me; I don't know why. I could see my face in his eyes. My eyes started to itch. I rubbed them. They were burning up. It felt like someone was slicing them. I squeezed my lids shut. ■ For fifteen days I lay in the bed that Mama and Papa and I slept in. Whenever I tried to open my eyes, I cried and the tears burned my skin. ■ Grandmother Pepita said I was going blind. She told me that Ana María, Papa's sister, was coming with her daughter Luz Marina.

She said not to be afraid, she'd sent for her to fix my eyes. ■ Everyone called Ana María Blind Ana because she'd lost her sight when she was a young woman. This was a punishment for lying about her father's death, Papa said. Mama said she could do black magic — that she could split her head and shoulders from the rest of her body and fly away like a hawk. I'd heard about witches that flew and people who made pacts with the Devil. I wondered about Ana María. ■ I heard a strange voice just outside the door. "Christians with pure blood and blond hair," the voice was saying, "don't live as long as black Christians. Look at my father. Who knows what's going happen to that child in there?" ■ I liked Blind Ana's voice. It crackled like the old victrola Grandfather Leónidas brought from Popayán. ■ "Can you give me some hot water for this child?" Blind Ana asked. ■ I heard water splash in the bucket as she came towards the bed. She asked me to sit up close to her. She felt me all over, especially my shoulders, my arms and my hands. She laughed. "Oh yes, you're a Vásquez! Yes, your shoulders will be wide and very strong. The only Vásquez trait you lack is tallness." ■ She pulled away the rag Mama had put over my eyes, then dipped her hands in water and touched my eyelids. ■ "Little girl, they told me that after your Papa looked in your eyes, your face broke out. They say your tears burned holes in your skin." ■ "Yes, Auntie." ■ Her fingers splashed in the water again. She began to sing: "Lord Jesus came to Bethlehem; the Devil walked out and God walked in. Saint Lucy, Virgin Martyr, by the power God has given you, save these little eyes from sin." ■ She wiped the crusts of dried tears from my eyes. "Now tell me, girl — can you open your eyes?" ■ I tried, but my eyelashes were still stuck together. ■ Three days and nights the tears streamed down my face. My hands broke out in sores. I couldn't eat. My skin was hot. ■ I heard Blind Ana say to Papa, "You tried to kill the child. You know your eyes are poison but you gave them to your daughter. God will punish you. The child is too sick. She's going to die." ■ They bathed me. Papa stayed up till the middle of the night taking care of me, giving me water, and Mama stayed with me until dawn. The neighbors came to keep them company. ■ I couldn't even move my head anymore. A stinking yellow pus oozed out of my eyes. Mama had to wipe them with a cloth every few minutes. They say my face looked eaten, as if someone had poured boiling water over it. My eyelashes had fallen out. And my hands were one big sore. ■ Finally Grandfather, who was very devoted to the Our Lady of the Sidewalks, said there was nothing else to do but ask her directly if I was going to get better, and when. If Our Lady of the Sidewalks said I was going to be blind, they told me later, then they should pray for God to take me, because what would a blind child do? ■ That was the faith their ancestors gave them. Whenever they needed a favor they asked Our Lady of the Sidewalks. She appeared to the poor farmers in Pasto. There were no roads then, no walkways. On full moon nights, with all the stars shining down, the flat rocks looked like a sidewalk. ■ One horrible rainy night, a man was carrying a load of potatoes and corn on his donkey when he came to the edge of a steep bluff. Just then the ground under the donkey split open. The man grabbed the lasso but the animal fell and he was left holding the broken rope. The man had a lot of children and he was very poor. When he saw the animal fall, he shouted, "Virgin Mary, help me!" It was very dark. He saw a light like a light bulb. ■ He scrambled down the mountain. When he got to the bottom where he thought the animal had fallen, he looked around to see if there was anything left of the corn or potatoes, or maybe just his saddle. His donkey was eating grass. And there was the Virgin — the man could see her perfectly now. He knelt down at her feet and cried and thanked her for doing him this favor. ■ But why did the Virgin appear here, everyone wondered. ■ There was a woman who had a daughter, a deaf mute. The woman carried the little girl everywhere on her back. One day she went to pick *churto*, a corn that's soft and sweet. It was getting dark. She was walking up the mountain with the little girl. She climbed slowly because she was carrying two sacks of corn and the child. Her mind was blank from exhaustion. The child said, "Mama, the *mestiza* is calling me." (It was what they called the people who were half-white and half-Indian.) This startled her poor mother. The little girl said it again, "The *mestiza* is calling me." ■ "Where is she?" her mother asked. The girl pointed straight ahead. And there was Our Lady of the Sidewalks. ■ So Mama and Papa got down on their knees at the foot of the bed. Mama said I already looked dead. Blind Ana had tried all her cures, herbs, and even a special water that they gave me with a little spoon, but I couldn't swallow it. So with tears in their eyes, as they say in story books, they asked Our Lady of the Sidewalks to cure their daughter or take her. They said Hail Marys and whatever else they could think of. ■ That night, at eleven o'clock, they say I stopped crying and became very still. ■ Mama and Papa had bought me a pink dress, so pretty. You couldn't tell where my skin left off and the dress began. They dressed me in the pretty pink dress and laid me out on the straw mattress. Mama sat on one side of the bed and Papa sat on the other, watching me, waiting for the hour of my death. They had spent three nights like this, they were worn out. Without realizing it they both fell asleep. ■ At five in the morning I woke up crying. My hands and face had cleared up. I managed to open my lids halfway. I saw a strip of adobe wall and Blind Ana's hands folded in prayer. I propped my eyelids up with my fingers. The room was blurry. Outside the little window I saw our green, green valley, the mountain behind it, and our neighbor's house with a red roof and smoke curling up. I saw their cows and hired hands with their hoes, planting the land, and our coffee bushes, weighed down with bright red berries, ready to harvest. ■ Everyone cried. All the neighbors came to look. People came from all over to see if it was true. It was really a miracle. No one doubted it. ■ "You must thank God every day of your life," Blind Ana said. "What is it like to see?" ■ I got out of bed and looked in the broken mirror Papa had brought from the city. It was shaped like an icicle in the Sierra Nevada. I got up close to it. I could see both my eyes at once. They were going from green to brown. They turned normal — just regular eyes with eyelashes. ■ Now that I could see, Blind Ana scared me. Her milky eyes were wide open, fixed on the cross I'd made out of laurel to keep the bad spirits away from our house. Blind Ana had a fuzzy black mustache and her brown hair was pulled back so tight that parts of her scalp stuck out. I looked around for Mama and Papa. ■ "Come sit with me, child," Blind Ana said. "I want to tell you what happened." She put her warm hand on mine. I shivered. "Your Papa feels ashamed but he couldn't help it. His strong wicked eyes were attracted to your pale eyes. By the time he knew what happened, it was too late. He had passed the power of evil from his eyes to yours. Now you must live with the burden of evil for the rest of your life." ■ I wanted to ask her what evil was, but she clamped her hand over my mouth. Her hands were dirty, they smelled like the earth. That smell — that must be what evil is.

High on a hill overlooking our valley, there was an old village where Spanish priests once lived. One of these priests, Father Ramos, died along with everyone else in the fire that destroyed the village, but before he died, he buried a treasure. The people of Magdalena said they could see Father Ramos walking on the hill. He used to bring young girls up there, give them a drink that made them lose their senses, then make them his slaves. ■ After the priest died, lots of people came to look for his lost gold. One day a man arrived with his thirteen little children and his donkey loaded with wood. Dusk fell as he looked for a place to spend the night. ■ The valley had been burned so the grass was like stubble on a man's shaved head. So instead of keeping to the path, the donkey started foraging to one side. The man followed his animal until he stumbled on something that sounded like metal. There was just enough light in the sky for him to see a big ring sticking up from the ground. He was sure it was the handle of Father Ramos's treasure chest. Here was the bronze handle just as the people had described it. ■ He was so happy he started to whistle. There was no one around, no houses or anything. "It's already too dark to start searching and digging now," he said to himself. He cleared the area around the ring and put a stick through it so he could find the spot again. ■ He had a buddy who loved money, and this buddy was my Uncle Luis. Uncle Luis made a fortune at the card table. As well as luck he had eyes that saw things the rest of us didn't. The man told Luis about his discovery. They cut bamboo poles to carry the chest, they got a sack and a crowbar and some food, and they set off. It was a long way, a good two-hour walk. When they got to the spot, they saw a light flaming up. Then it flickered and disappeared. ■ They started digging and soon they hit a gigantic trunk. The moon was shining. The man asked Luis to go to the woods to cut a pole to hook the handle with so they could pull out the trunk. Luis was scared; he was scared of the woods, scared of the night, and scared of snakes. But Uncle Luis was not so scared when he got to thinking about robbing the man. ■ The man wasn't there when he returned with the pole. Luis slipped the top off the trunk and reached inside. Yes, there were coins. He snuck away to get the sack he'd left in the forest. He tried to untie the knot he'd tied at the top of the sack, but he got scared of the dark and he went back to the stake, where at least there was moonlight. ■ "What are you up to?" the man called from the shadows. ■ "Here? Just screwing around trying to loosen this knot." ■ The man came and opened the chest to see for himself. When the lid slid to the ground, there was a sound like silverware falling: CLANK! The chest sank into the earth like into a deep puddle. ■ They got scared and went home. The next day they went back to the spot where Luis thought he'd stuck the stick, but they couldn't see a thing.

Grandfather Leónidas, my mother's father, managed a lot of coffee plantations in the area. He got people together to start their own market so they could buy things right there instead of going all the way to the blacks' market, a day's ride to the river. (Many, many years ago the Spanish brought the blacks to El Valle, the province in which our valley was located, to mine the gold in the river.) The first thing Grandfather did was bring water from the waterfalls on the mountain. And as soon as there was water, people came to buy land from the black people. Then they fixed the roads so people could come to trade. They cleared the jungle and planted corn, bananas, and coffee. They built a little schoolhouse. Then Grandfather went to Popayán to ask the priest to preside at the opening ceremonies for the village. Everyone from up and down the Patía River came. ■ Grandfather stuck to panning gold in the river and he was forever running into foreign prospectors. They'd go out with a hollowed-out piece of cane to get a sample of the dirt. If that looked good, they'd start making big holes all over the place. ■ Some Americans struck gold on the Zajando River. They came with dredges and black workers from the plains of Patía to work the river by hand. It's a tropical country; the heat burns. The Americans built beautiful houses with fans in a separate place that no one could enter and they had cars that they drove along the riverbank. ■ They took out gold by the ton. Some of the blacks got rich stealing. The Americans caught on and brought in gold detectors. They found gold in the blacks' mouths, ears, hair, and clothes. Some of them had even swallowed it. ■ The Americans took so much gold out of the river, they took it out in bars. Then they went away and abandoned the dredges. Now, during the winter rains, the river doesn't rise and flood the fields like it used to; the force of the gold is gone. ■ The land dried up in places. No one replanted the trees and bushes, so by the time I was born the place was a patchwork of desert and dark-green, tree-filled spaces; you could see in one glance the change of the landscape from the lush valley the Spaniards found to the dust and cactuses of today. ■ This worn-out valley, like so many villages Grandfather told me about, coughs up its young people — the ones who make the progress — to the city; the children and the old people are left to be educated and nurtured by the trees and the animals. The old women who stay behind look like they've grown back down into the earth: they wrap themselves in layers of dark clothes, so you can no longer see the shape of their bodies; only their eyes and noses and part of their mouths. ■ Mama lived on a farm called the Pantry (nowadays it's called Hope). In the black dirt the manioc grew as long as Mama's arm. Grandfather's house was huge and so was the store. Ever since I can remember Grandfather had a store. The big storeroom was filled to the top with rice that needed to be husked. Mama pounded it with a huge wooden mortar to loosen the brown shells around the kernels. The corn had just been harvested then; it was dry but still on the cob, and it was piled up in the granary. In another room Grandfather kept medicine and things like that — alcohol, gasoline, kerosene. ■ Mama slept on the other side of the house with some of her brothers and sisters. Uncle Marcos was still a baby. They had a lot of animals: Mama had a beautiful cat Grandfather gave her. Grandmother had a sewing machine and she kept a big brood of guinea pigs in the kitchen — Grandfather brought them from Pasto. They were grey and their eyes were red. He dug a ditch to the house from the pools in the mountain, so the family had water. ■ It was dawn. Everyone was still sleeping. Grandfather was away building a house for Señora Villanueva in a settlement called The Watering Hole. Only Grandmother, the baby and Mama were at home. Grandmother screamed, "María, get up! We're on fire!" Mama said she opened her eyes and the room was lit up. She ran out to the banana field after Grandmother, who had Uncle Marcos in one arm and her sewing machine in the other. ■ It was too late to save anything. The straw roof went up in a second. Mama's cat had just had kittens and she said she could hear them crying through the buzzing of the flames. Some of the guinea pigs got out, but most of them burned up with the chickens. Mama stood in the middle of the banana plants with Grandmother, watching everything they owned go up in smoke. ■ It was my great-grandmother's husband, Pedro, that started the fire. Great-grandmother had money and animals from her first husband. Pedro had been living with her for awhile, but my uncles, her oldest sons, caught him stealing. When Pedro saw they were about to throw him out, he asked my great-grandmother to marry him, which she did. ■ Then one night Pedro came home drunk as usual, and slammed my great-grandmother against the wall. When she came to, she vomited blood. She got sicker and sicker and in two months she died. Grandfather went after Pedro with a knife. But Pedro ran away like a rabbit and yelled, "Your house will burn down." And it happened just as he said.

El Valle is coffee land. By February the coffee branches are filled with berries getting ripe. You pick them so the ripe ones don't fall to the ground. This is called graining. In April there is a final, smaller harvest. There are six pickings every year. Then the plants bloom again. ■ When you pick coffee, some of the berries always fall on the ground, and later they sprout. When you weed the plants, you look for these sprouts and gently pack dirt around them so they'll grow. When they get big enough, you transplant them. ■ You gather the coffee in a basket tied to your waist. You walk up and down picking the berries until it's full. Then you dump the beans into a sack. You try to fill your sack faster than anybody else and not let any berries fall to the ground, or grab any green berries. You dump your sack in a big box where the pulp is taken off. The next day you wash the coffee and dry it until you can pick off the shell (shells make the coffee bitter). Then you pick out the broken seeds and take the rest to the village to sell. ■ Mama used to work on other people's farms too. There were great big houses where they all slept in a big attic, thirty or forty kids. Everyone was decent — no fooling around when the lights went out. If you were caught fooling around, you wouldn't get work. ■ During the coffee harvest a lot of blacks came south. Mama told me a story about a beautiful black woman, Berta, who had a daughter by a white man in El Bordo, and a son by the owner of a farm near us; this man was black. One of the single men fell in love with Berta. They went off to live together but her mother didn't like this guy because he was poor. Berta continued to live with him anyway. Her mother told him to leave town or she was going to kill him. He didn't pay any attention to her. ■ When the coffee harvest came around again, everyone went to weed the plants one last time — the black migrants and the regular workers. Berta's mother was with them. While they were resting, she slipped something into the black guy's drink. The next morning his stomach began to bother him, and by afternoon it was so swelled up he couldn't fit through the door to the barn. He was a tall man. It was a horrible sight to see this giant with a balloon for a stomach. He looked about to explode. ■ Four coffee pickers carried him to Don Arturo, the herb doctor. Mama said Don Arturo was an old Indian man, very tiny, very charming. He started pulling things out of a sack: two cats' skulls, a rabbit skull, the eye-tooth of a tiger, bulls' eyes, and flat round red seeds with black spots in the middle. Then he brought out a big enamelled bowl and a stick with a knot in it that he used for a mallet. He put the things from the sack in the middle of the bowl and pounded them with the mallet until they were crushed finely. When Don Arturo got tired Mama pitched in. Everyone was saying the black guy was going to pop like a balloon and die. ■ Don Arturo dumped the bone dust into boiling water and added three big stones — white, black and brown. When the water had nearly boiled away he emptied the contents onto a clay plate, covered it with a board, and made a bed for the black guy out of animal skins. ■ The poor man was shouting in pain and foaming at the mouth. They laid him down and covered him with herbs. Don Arturo lit some incense and asked us to grab an edge of the cow skin and lift the black guy up while he recited a prayer and sprinkled herbs. By then the potion had cooled down. He hit the guy on the side of the head to knock the demon out of him and then made him drink the bone broth. As soon as the guy got the drink down, he started to sweat, then he fainted. ■ Don Arturo asked everyone there to be silent and hold hands and kneel in a circle around him. It was night by now, and the black guy's stomach was shrinking. He came to and asked to go to the bathroom. The men sat him up in a giant gourd that Don Arturo had picked from his gourd tree. His stomach spread out on the floor like a cloth. He lost control of his bowels. All the evil gas inside expanded until it exploded. Mama said it sounded like someone fired a shotgun. The black guy fainted again. "Lie him back down," Don Arturo said. The fire blazed. He covered him with skins and began to pray again. After eight days with Don Arturo, the black guy's stomach returned to normal. ■ The coffee fields were about a half-day walk up the mountain. Every morning Mama used to climb up carrying the workers' food in pots and pans. And she cooked for them in the field. At night they brought the coffee down to the house and peeled it and washed it and sorted it. They sold it to a buyer who lived in Santa Cruz and another one in San Alfonso. These rich men lent them a lot of money to buy food and things they needed. As soon as they began to pick the coffee, the rich men came for their money. There wasn't very much left. One year the crop would be very good, the next year it might be horrible or maybe just average. You knew how much your land would produce; you could tell if it was going to be a good crop or a bad crop. On the basis of that, they lent you a certain amount of money. When the coffee was ready, it belonged to the money man. It seemed the people with money avoided real work and took advantage of the others. ■ Take the case of Estanislao Navía, for example. He was a friend of Grandfather's. He was about thirty years old, solid-looking, very nice, a hard worker. He moved his family to El Valle and got work with a big landowner, one of those fat, rich, rotten ones. Sergio Ibarra was his name. Estanislao turned the farm into a very profitable place. He was a good boss. He treated people well; everybody wanted to work there. The coffee bushes were bent to the ground with berries. Those were very good years. ■ Sergio Ibarra hardly ever went to the farm. He sent his lazy sons who didn't know anything about agriculture or work or anything except hanging around. ■ Sergio agreed to pay

Estanislao half the profits after two years. But when Sergio figured out just how much this amounted to, he hired a peasant to kill Estanislao, because he preferred to have him murdered rather than pay him for his work. ■ Sergio's cronies invited Estanislao to go drinking. Estanislao didn't drink. He'd go to Santa Cruz to buy meat and supplies and then he'd head right back to the farm. Just to be friendly he drank two beers. They insisted, he had to have a real drink. He realized it was five-thirty and he had an hour's walk ahead of him. Sergio Ibarra begged him to stay. Estanislao had a whiskey to oblige Sergio, then he left. ■ It was dark now, darker than it was light. The killer watched Estanislao leave. He let him walk about a half-block, then stabbed him thirty-seven times. No part of him was left untouched. Those days, big knives were in style, and they used them like a sword or a bayonet. ■ They couldn't bury him until the judge came across the river to see the body and officially declare him dead. But it was a terrible winter; the Patía River was high and the horses couldn't get across because there was no bridge. Estanislao's body lay for a week in the Santa Cruz saloon. ■ My uncle's father-in-law was the owner of the place. Mama went down to look at him one night. Everyone brought candles. The place was packed. She said she was shocked to see such a healthy and good person die like that, sliced to pieces — to see how cruel people could be. You couldn't get too close; the smell was horrible. His body was bloated. All thirty-seven wounds were open and crawling with worms. ■ He lay there until the judge came to certify the details of the crime — or the accident, as the judge, who was an old friend of Sergio Ibarra's, called it. ■ They were supposed to take Estanislao to El Bordo for the autopsy but the river was still running too high. There was water everywhere, so they took him by another route along the Olaya River. They couldn't make it all the way to the cemetery because the smell was too much, so they buried him on the river bank. ■ Sergio Ibarra evicted Estanislao Navía's wife and two kids. The farms were abandoned. The coffee was finished.

I was always happy to see Papa coming home across the valley because he would pick me up and I could look very far down to the ground; he was so tall. Sometimes, holding me and tossing me way up high, he told me strange sad stories. ■ "All people are the same, Alicia; we come from one line because the earth is round. But you and I, Alicita, we have what is called a debt with destiny. We must pay for things that dead people have done. No one knows where it will end. ■ "They say the Vásquez family has some Spanish blood in it, that our roots are diseased. The Spaniards were bad people who came here to kill and to steal what belonged to the Indians, the valley people. They made dark magic with their blue eyes and light skin. Now the Vásquez tree is almost dead. There are only a few of us left. ■ "Your grandfather, Marco Tulio, was an unusual man. He rode into El Valle from the north — Antioquia, where the rich people lived. No one had seen anyone like him. He had light skin, blue eyes and a long brown mustache. He wore a suit; the men in the valley never wore anything but baggy pants and ponchos. ■ "Marco Tulio's brain was powerful, more powerful even than the priest's. He made trades — chickens for pigs, sheep for donkeys, donkeys for land — until everything was his. He took things that were other people's birthright. The valley people didn't like that. 'We're poor people,' they said. 'We're only clay; our way is to make a living by the sweat of our brows.' ■ "One day a log came floating down the river. On this log sat a carpenter bird. A young boy from over the mountain was standing next to the bank. He looked at the beautiful bird and he looked at it and looked at it. The sun began to go down; still he looked at it. He'd been bewitched by the blue and orange bird with black eyes; he couldn't look at anything else, and finally the gaze of the bird's black eyes blinded him. When the boy could no longer see, he reached out to touch the feathers of the carpenter bird, but instead his fingers touched the beaded leather of Marco Tulio's machete case. He heard your grandfather laugh. Marco Tulio took him by the shoulders and turned him toward the mountain." ■ "His eyes were very powerful, weren't they, Papa? But why did he want to blind the boy?" ■ "The boy's father had refused to sell him some pigs and he wouldn't let anyone get away with refusing him anything. The valley people took notice. They said Marco Tulio had rage in his eyes. Pigs, dogs, chickens — when they saw him, they went stiff and fell over and died." ■ "But I don't understand, Papa. What did Marco Tulio do except become a rich man? At least he got what he wanted. I wish I could learn to do what my grandfather did." ■ When my mother's father, my grandfather Leónidas, was eighteen, he left El Valle to walk around the world with my grandfather Marco Tulio. They packed big sacks of clothes and potions against snake bite. They walked all day, stopping at dusk to cut poles for their tent. For years they traveled this way. ■ Marco Tulio had come from Antioquia, the department of Medellín, which is now the home of the drug lords. The Antioqueños have always worked hard and traveled in search of their fortunes. Even so Marco Tulio was unusual. He learned witchcraft from the Indians; Grandfather Leónidas learned how to build houses and weave baskets and carve spoons. I'm not sure if they returned to El Valle together. Anyway, Grandfather Leónidas came back when he was thirty-nine and got married. Grandmother Pepita was only seventeen. ■ Grandfather kept one of Marco Tulio's magic books locked in a chest. When their house burned down, the time Great-grandmother's husband was making mischief, the magic book burned with it. Grandmother said the fire was really God's punishment for keeping that book. ■ Grandfather Leónidas never hurt a living soul. He used what he learned to do good. For example, in the mountains there is a plant called *hiraca*. People use it to thatch roofs, but if you cut it during the wrong phase of the moon it sprouts caterpillars that eat the leaves till only the veins are left. Whenever Grandfather saw the butterflies, he'd whack the house with a pole and recite some magic words till the caterpillars crawled away. ■ But Marco Tulio was terrible. Papa inherited the Evil Eye from him, but he didn't have eyes that could kill, only make somebody very sick and maybe eventually die. That's what they call the Stupid Eye and that's what I have. But people like Marco Tulio could look at you and in two or three days you'd be dead. ■ He was short like my Grandfather Leónidas but skinny, so when he mounted his horse, he looked like a monkey on top of an elephant. People would bring him their horses to break in. It's a pretty rough job, but Marco Tulio, he just slung a lasso around the horse's neck and yanked it from side to side and hopped on, bareback. ■ It took a while for word to get around that he was a sorcerer; most people thought he was just a healer. He'd buy a horse or cow from someone he wanted to cast a spell on. The person would get sick. Marco Tulio would ask his neighbors how his victim was feeling. Soon the sick person would send for Marco Tulio. Marco Tulio would cure him right away and collect another couple of cows in payment. He got very, very rich. By the time he died, he had seventeen hundred head of cattle, and it took three sacks of salt to feed them every day. ■ There was a witch called Antonina who lived just down the mountain from him, and she also worked a lot of bad magic. One day everyone got together to clear the forest and plant corn. They made *chicha*, the fiery corn liquor the Indians made, and slaughtered a hog and danced to guitars. Antonina was a young girl at the time and Marco Tulio couldn't have been more than twenty-five. He fell in love with her but she was married. He proposed to her anyway. When she turned him down, he said, "I'm going to give you a stomach ache that will kill you." ■ "If you give me a stomach ache," Antonina said, "I'll break your leg. We'll see who knows more magic." ■ They sat face to face drinking *chicha* from a big gourd. She carried her magic things in a little bag around her neck and he carried his tied to his belt. She gave him a wicked look and recited a spell. ■ A pain shot through his foot. "You slut," he said, "I'm going to put a rattlesnake in your belly." ■ First he got rid of the pain in his foot. Then he brought out his shells and arranged them in a circle to protect himself against anything else she might try. ■ He whisked her up — she was a thin, delicate woman — and while they were dancing, she collapsed. Her belly sloshed from side to side, getting bigger each second. She screamed and begged him not to kill her. ■ "Don't worry, Antonina," Marco Tulio cackled. "Nothing is going to happen to you." ■ Everybody kept drinking and dancing. ■ At dawn she was still on the floor, almost dead by now. Her stomach was as big as a basket of corn and she'd peed all over her clothes. So she offered Marco Tulio her four most beautiful cows and sent her sisters to get them.

After Marco Tulio tethered the cows, he turned Antonina back to normal. ■ "Just don't come around casting any more spells on me," he said. "You don't know who you're dealing with. If you want to die, keep on pestering me." ■ So they made a truce and became friends and instead of casting spells on each other they got together and bewitched other people. Right after Marco Tulio was murdered, Antonina died — an old woman, all wrinkled up like she'd been kept under water too long. Maybe the wrinkles were the last spell he cast on her. ■ Marco Tulio was getting on in years by the time he got married. Grandmother Liliana was from Santa Cruz. A missionary from Popayán performed the ceremony. There was a big party with lots of fireworks and *aguardiente*, a licorice-tasting brandy they make from sugarcane. They cooked rice and meat and *tamales* and candy. They slaughtered twenty chickens and stewed them in a huge pot. The missionary said mass, then went to sleep while everybody danced all night and into the morning. ■ While Grandmother Liliana helped carry one of the saints in the Sunday procession the next day, Marco Tulio was still drinking with his buddies. The procession passed the bar where they'd been all night. Marco Tulio started yelling that his wife was licking the missionary's ass, that they were lovers. He punched the missionary and grabbed Grandmother Liliana by the hair and dragged her through the street. The missionary told Marco Tulio that this was no way to treat his bride: "Slavery was abolished a long time ago, sir." Marco Tulio went to punch him again but the crowd held him back. The missionary knelt in the middle of the street. "My curse on you," he said, "and on your children's children." ■ I've heard the valley people say that Marco Tulio was an animal; he didn't believe in God. "If God exists," he said, "show him to me." But somehow he got an idea to visit his parents way up north, and they were Catholics. "How can you go to your parents' house," Grandmother Liliana asked, "and present your children like horses or calves you traded for? You've got to get them baptised so you can introduce them by their Christian names." ■ So he brought his children to be baptised. There were six of them: Elías, Julián (my father), Ana María, Mercedes, Ana Julia, and Armida. It looked like a caravan. The horses were gigantic and gorgeous. Marco Tulio was so short he had to use the fence as a stepladder to dismount. The whole village crowded into the hut that was the school and the church. They all went to watch because it was so strange, all these grown children being baptised. ■ Marco Tulio decided to first visit his parents by himself and just show them pictures of his children. He had his picture taken with Uncle Elías, his oldest son, standing in the park, Uncle Elías wearing his army uniform and Marco Tulio with his tweed suit, looking very serious. After that Marco Tulio decided he could take the kids one at a time until the grandparents had met all of them. But this was one dream he never lived to accomplish. ■ Marco Tulio was a cruel man. He liked to hang his children by their wrists and whip them until their backs streamed blood. Grandmother Liliana — he just slapped her in the face. I guess it made him feel good to beat my aunts and uncles. He whipped them if they were late running errands. He whipped them if they didn't pick enough coffee. If one of the animals slipped and fell over the cliff, he nearly beat them to death. The kids went to work at five in the morning, came home for lunch, left to work again, came back home at six, and went to bed. They were slaves. When they saw Marco Tulio riding across the valley, they started to shake inside. ■ He spoke very little. It was as if he was always listening for the sound of his death. Once, in Pan de Azúcar, when he was drunk, he got stabbed twenty-seven times — but he survived. The man was worse than weeds. Another time they cut him and he got gangrene in the arm. His flesh rotted and fell away, but he glued it back. He was like a fish or something. ■ His son came home from the army — Uncle Elías, the eldest, the one in the picture. He waited till the workers had left and everyone was asleep. Marco Tulio was sleeping face-down on his big balsa-wood pillow, which was filled with *peso* notes. (He also kept two pails full of coins under his bed.) Grandmother Liliana and Aunt Ana María were lying next to him. ■ Uncle Elías came in with an oil lamp and forced Grandmother Liliana to hold it. Then he let Marco Tulio have it with an axe. With the first blow, Grandfather got up, screaming and moaning. Uncle Elías hit him again and he went down. He managed to say, "Don't kill me, son. For God's sake, don't kill me. Take the money, take it. But don't kill me." ■ Uncle Elías cut off both his hands just above the wrist. Then he finished him off with the axe. In the light of the lamp, you could see Marco Tulio's brains splatter the wall, Aunt Ana María said. Uncle Elías held a knife to Grandmother Liliana, and to Ana María, and said that if they talked, he'd kill them and the rest of the family, too. The workers and the children who slept in the attic, they came. Uncle Elías nicked every one of them on the neck with his knife and made them swear not to talk. "What I did to my father is nothing," he said. ■ Uncle Elías told the workers to dig a grave near the garden. It was only the family that watched as they put the body in the hole. Then Uncle Elías spread the news that robbers must have broken into the house and killed his father when he refused to give up his money. ■ The next week Grandmother went to the priest and confessed that the night after Marco Tulio died, she'd seen him riding his horse in the garden, tending his magical plants, groaning, "My children. . . my wife. . . this garden. . . my farm. . . ," and that now she saw him all the time, and that she was afraid. ■ The priest said the garden had to be destroyed. He gave her a bottle of holy water and told her to sprinkle it all around. The first holy day after Marco Tulio died, the rain washed away all his plants. And then new plants were born, but not the same ones. ■ The police came and took Uncle Elías to the judge. How could he not have seen what happened, the judge asked, and why didn't he come to his father's defense? Uncle Elías said: "May a rattlesnake bite me if I saw who killed my father!" ■ The judge told my Aunt Ana María that if she, sleeping in the same bed, said she was asleep and didn't see anything. . . that was impossible! She would have had to be dead not to have realized what was going on. She said, "May God take away my sight if I saw who killed my father!" ■ People began to ask questions. Two of the workers were arrested. They kept them in jail for a while and then they disappeared. Uncle Elías paid to have them let them go. ■ Years later, on one of our trips back to El Valle, we had to go on horseback from El Bordo. My older brother Javier didn't like riding. "Mama, get me off this animal," he cried. "I want to ride in a taxi. . . ." We came to a giant hill and Mama saw someone coming and she knew we were going to meet at a very wide part, the kind that forms when so many horses pass by. ■ Mama recognized Uncle Elías riding along, very distracted, she said, looking a lot like Marco Tulio with his dark coffee eyes, riding a very fine horse, an ivory horse with a new saddle and bridle. The saddle was so elegant, and the chaps, too. He was wearing his revolver and machete. ■ We were riding Grandmother Pepita's horse, a white horse called Pig Soup. All the way from Santa Cruz to Pan de Azúcar, we hadn't met up with a single soul, not before we saw Uncle Elías. ■ Mama had taken him to court about Papa's coffee trees. (Uncle Elías had said they were his and sold the coffee from them.) He never forgave her that. How could a woman take money away from him — a mere woman? He swore she'd never get away with it. But Mama said, "God's will be done. We won't turn back." ■ We came together at the crossroads. He acted surprised. His hand went to his revolver. He said, "How's it going, little sister-in-law? How are the children? Where are you headed?" Mama told him we were going to my grandmother's, so he said: "I'm on my way to Santa Cruz. I'll be seeing you." ■ Mama said she thought he was going to shoot her in the back. But no, we never saw him again. ■ He bought a farm with the money from Marco Tulio's pillow. He bought two huge farms, in fact, with lots of cattle. He married a very wealthy woman, but she never went to the farm, just stayed in her own town. So when it came time for the coffee harvest, Uncle Elías found himself alone, sleeping in the attic. ■ One night he went downstairs to relieve himself. On his way back to bed, something bit his foot. He took another step and got bitten again. He went upstairs to get a light and then downstairs and yes sir, there was a rattler. He was a dead man. ■ And Aunt Ana María — the daughter that said she didn't see anything but if she did, may God take away her sight — that was Blind Ana. Aunt Ana María had a coffee plantation way up in the mountains where she'd gone to live with one of her father's workers. I don't know how many days it'd been since she'd given birth to her last child — it was a girl, Luz Marina. Anyway her husband made her cook for the workers. So she went with her baby and a horse laden with pots and everything. It was very hot and she had to cross over a ravine. Suddenly she felt as if someone had hit her in the eyes. She covered her face and when she took her hands away she couldn't see. Then she was able to see a little but it was like railroad tracks were crossing inside her head. She managed to make lunch but later, going back home, she couldn't see anything and her eyes were shining in a beautiful but horrible way; they were like pools of blood. ■ When Marco Tulio died, Grandmother Liliana was pregnant with her last child; she died in childbirth. My aunts and uncles became orphans. The livestock died. There were debts. The property was sold off. The males took to wandering. When they finished Marco Tulio, they finished everything. They were a big family and they were cruel.

Mama brought me up not to go looking for bad thoughts, and if I had any, to pray. She always said there was a devil inside me. ■ I couldn't understand why; I couldn't fly like witches do. "God, please forgive me," I prayed. "I am good, God." I decided I wasn't going to look at anybody with my Evil Eye, I was only going to pray and think about God. But the idea of the Devil wouldn't leave me. So many thousand things came into my head, I couldn't keep track of them all. I was curious about the Devil. I wanted to know what he looked like. Did he smell like dirt? ■ One summer day Mama and Papa and Javier went to the village. They left me at home because I wasn't old enough yet to help with the market; Papa had to carry me when my feet got tired. Mama told me to get in bed and stay there till they returned. Then she tied the door shut. ■ I was drawing a big tree with every different kind of bird I could think of in it, when I heard Blind Ana call, "Oh, house, is anyone there?" ■ "Yes, Aunt, it's me, Alicia. Please come in. You have to untwist the wire." ■ Blind Ana lived with her daughter, Luz Marina, whose father went to fight in the war with Perú and never came back. Luz Marina was rebellious, Blind Ana said, because she was born while her father was fighting. But Blind Ana had been wild herself and one day during a fight about who was going to milk the heifer, she called Luz Marina a whore and dragged her out of the house by her long black braids. Luz Marina was deeply offended and, although she was only thirteen years old, she ran away, leaving Blind Ana to fend for herself. So she had to sell the heifer and learn to get around completely by smells, sounds, and touch. She talked about putting a curse on Luz Marina but then a letter came, postmarked Bogotá.

I take up this pencil and paper and greet you and tell you the following. ❧ I am working in a house in Bogotá. The master and mistress are North Americans. I take care of their two daughters and sleep on a piece of soft foam in the kitchen. I hope you don't feel betrayed, Mama, but I am going to stay here. I know my soul isn't for sale, not yet. ❧ *Don't put a curse on me, because if you curse me, something could happen, an accident or a crash. I ask you to pray that I will be spared from all evil and danger.* ❧ *And Mama, I am a little sick. I think it is the wound from when the bull gored me that is bothering me because sometimes my back feels very bad. Anyway, I have to tell you the following — that I will visit you in these same months of May. Wait for the next letter I will write you. I hope you aren't displeased.* ❧ *Well, Mama, I must say goodbye to you. When I go to the house, we will talk about more things, and when I arrive I hope you'll have lots of cheeses, chickens, hens' eggs, and lots of little baby turkeys. I say goodbye to my mother now. Don't be sad because you are alone. I send you lots of kisses because I don't have anything else to send you. Here, I send you all these kisses — 1 2 3 4 5 6 7 8 9 10, up to 10,000 kisses, and hugs. Bye, Mama.*

Yours,

Luz Marina Vásquez Moreno

P. S. Lots of kisses to my flower, Animolio, the one I planted in the garden before I left, and kisses also to my dogs, Curi and Cariño, and to my dear goat, Sweet Heart, and to you, little Mama.

Blind Ana was pleased to get the letter, which was bordered by little hearts inside big ones and the phrase: "My heart is in my Mama's." She hoped she could lure Luz Marina back to the farm. She sent for my mama to dictate a reply.

I take up the pen to send you my warmest greetings. I hope this letter finds you well. That is what my heart desires and thinks of every moment. Greetings to all your people there. I hope this letter finds them well too. I will go on to tell you the following — that I will wait for you on my birthday, the 30th of May and that I am still sick. I want very much to be happy on my birthday so send me word on what day you will come. I received your little letter. Thank you very much. I hope God blesses you because of what you have sent me. Up till now everything is fine here. Lots of greetings from the goats and hundreds of kisses from the little turkeys. Give my hugs and kisses to the children. When will you bring them for me to see?

Luz Marina bought a present for Blind Ana's birthday — a piece of glass to cover the window hole next to her bed and keep the wind from chilling her. She held it carefully on her lap all during the twenty-six hour bus ride from Bogotá. ■ Blind Ana was proud of the glass window; it was the only one in all the valley. As soon as she got up in the morning she pressed her palm and fingertips flat against it. When the sun was shining, the glass got almost hot. Blind Ana's touch was so sensitive she could tell by the temperature of the glass whether it was noon or two p.m., if it was September or November, or if it was going to rain. ■ I heard Blind Ana patting the door as she tried to find the latch. "Ah, good. I wanted to see how you were getting along, Alicita." ■ "My eyes don't burn and I'm getting taller each day." ■ "Ah, I'm glad, child." ■ She opened the door and guided herself into the room with the wooden staff she used to herd cattle. Her bright blue plastic boots were covered with mud. She wore a man's green jacket and a black wool skirt. ■ "Look Alicita, this is my wedding skirt. Manuel the tailor made a whole wardrobe for me — a white dress, this skirt and a matching jacket." She smoothed the crumpled skirt and pointed to the big oval patches above the hemline. "This is where the rats ate." She laughed and touched her crotch. "What if they'd eaten higher up?" ■ "Would you like some coffee, Auntie?" ■ "Yes. I have such a thirst it could kill a cow. Get the fire going." ■ I built a little fire. I was so small I could barely reach the hearth, so I had to bring a stone to stand on. The dried eucalyptus leaves flamed up. Blind Ana sat on the bed. She held out her right hand. I pressed the coffee into her hand until she got a grip on it. I sat down on the bed next to her. ■ "Did you know my mama when she was a little girl? Was she like me?" ■ "No, Alicia, your mama and her family, they are a different story. They are Indians, not light-skinned like you and your Papa. Your mama was a smart one. If María heard a joke or a poem or something, she had it memorized right away. When they brought the first sewing machine to the village, she was eleven years old. She figured out how to take it apart, she saw how it worked, and how to make something with it. Before she married, she learned to sew and embroider. Nobody taught her. ■ "But María wouldn't even make coffee. Now and then she helped with the washing, that's all. She traveled to Cali, Popayán — such great cities — wherever she wanted, before she got married. She sold everything she sewed. She bought earrings, rings, tiaras. At home she sold soda and cigarettes. I bought the first sodas I ever tasted from her. She was a girl who enjoyed life. She should look after you the same way she was looked after." ■ Blind Ana leaned over the bed and spat out the juice of the coca leaves she was chewing. ■ "Your mama was your grandfather's favorite. No one ever raised a finger against María without Leónidas knowing it. He took her on trips with him, and there weren't many girls who got to leave the village. I never left till I was forty. But María — no one ever told her what to do. ■ "One day María was waiting on customers in her little store. I was there to buy salt. Pepita, her mother, came in. 'María,' she said, 'go turn over the *arepas* (the fried maize cakes that she made better than anyone else) or they'll burn; they'll be nothing but charcoal. Pay attention, now.' ■ "María didn't answer. Pepita thought that, as insolent as María was, she would at least turn over the *arepas*, but when she went to the kitchen the *arepas* were burned to ashes. Pepita shouted, 'María, do you think this is right?' She grabbed the hot *arepas* and mashed them in María's face. ■ "When your grandfather Leónidas came home eight days later, María complained to him. Leónidas didn't say a word, he just grabbed his rifle. Pepita dropped to the floor, the shots smashed into the wall behind her." ■ "Auntie, why do I have the Evil Eye instead of my brother Javier?" ■ "Well, maybe it's because you and your papa look so much alike. Your eyes are strong. A child who looks at you will get a stomach ache. You must learn to prevent that: make the sign of the cross with your saliva on his neck and burn a strand of your hair and put the ashes on his belly button and pray. The thing is, the Evil Eye is given to people who are different. . . ." ■ Blind Ana's nephew Luis called from the pasture. "Aunt, we have to go." ■ "Come and have some coffee first, Luis." ■ Luis was beautiful. He had bright blue eyes. I poured him a cup of coffee and he took it outside to drink under the plantain tree. ■ Blind Ana put her finger to my right eye. "Remember, you have too much energy in your eyes." ■ I started looking at everyone's eyes, at children and adults, the nuns, everyone I saw. I wanted to ask them if they had bad eyes, but I was too shy to open my mouth.

Mama fixed my papa's trousers before she ever laid eyes on him. Mama's brother, Uncle Luis, had married Papa's sister, Ana Julia, and they had two kids. They split up when Uncle Luis got drafted. But before that, Mama used to visit them and mend the boys' work clothes. ■ One day while Mama was picking corn in the rain, she heard a horse galloping across the river. The rider was a huge man with light skin and curly hair. ■ He found his pants neatly mended. Ana Julia told him that Luis's pretty, hard-working sister sewed them. That night he hung around for the coffee grinding. ■ Mama went to town with Grandfather Leónidas and took orders to make dresses. When she delivered the clothes to the village a week later, she saw Papa again, sitting on his big fine horse, wearing a new pair of blue tweed pants and fancy shoes. He dismounted, and said, "How do you do, Miss María. I want to marry you." ■ "Oh, but you are very forward," she said. "You really ought to look for another woman because I'm not ready to get married." ■ "I'm going to marry you." ■ "I don't think so." ■ He touched her arm with his chilly fingers. "We'll see about that." ■ Grandfather Leónidas told Papa he wouldn't allow it. Papa said he was going to marry Mama anyway. He had everything arranged, even the priest. ■ Grandfather took her to Cali, but Papa found her and brought her home to get married. Now he asked Grandmother Pepita if he could marry her. Grandmother didn't think it was a good idea for Mama to go off with a man who had no mother or father. ■ "Now look, Julián," she said, "a young man like you shouldn't bother with a dark-skinned girl like María; she's just an ugly little thing, and poor. You are a fine young man with a future. You're single, you have everything you want. But marriage. . . you don't look like a husband. Think about it." ■ When Grandmother realized she couldn't stop them, she said, "Getting married is getting married and nothing else." But Grandmother said Mama was too spoiled to know what she was talking about. ■ When Mama knelt down for Grandmother's blessing,

Grandmother said that if she married Papa she was no daughter of hers. Grandmother really wanted her to marry a boy who'd come from the city to spray the fields during an ant infestation, but this boy was a Conservative and Grandfather was a Liberal. ■ Mama and Papa got married in El Bordo on the feast of Our Lady of Mercy. Twenty-five couples waited in the church. The priest recited the vows one by one and by the time her turn came, Mama was trembling. Standing by Papa's side at the altar, she didn't even reach his shoulder. ■ Afterwards they went to the place called Sitting Stone, a big flat field where the blacks had a tent-market. Papa bought lots of things — blankets, sheets, and beautiful pots. The next morning they were up at five and on their way to Grandmother's house to get Mama's things. Mama said that when she looked for Grandmother, she was nowhere around. But Grandmother said Mama and Papa didn't even go to their own wedding party; they left Grandmother and Grandfather with the dinner all laid out. Blind Ana said Mama took everything she could — chickens, everything. From outside the house she yelled, "See you later," and that was that until Grandmother went up the mountain to visit her when she heard she got sick. It never occurred to Grandfather that Mama would marry without his permission. He got sadder and sadder till it started affecting his mind. All he could say was, "My fate. . . , the fate of my daughter. My fate. . . , the fate of my daughter." ■ Mama's four sisters ate the wedding lunch. Papa was so pleased with himself about getting married, he'd hired Uncle Luis to make four new beds. It was the first time they'd been together. Papa tried to be affectionate, but Mama said every time he stepped into the bedroom, her hair stuck up and she got goosebumps all over. Fifteen days later, she still didn't want to lay with him. ■ "Why did you tell me you were never going to get married?" he asked with a mocking, wounding smile. ■ "Getting married never crossed my mind." ■ "So how come you did?" ■ "Maybe God planned it?" ■ He burst out laughing. "What God? You said you were not going to get married. You despised me. You had big ideas because you were the daughter of a rich man. You didn't want to dirty your hands." ■ "See, it's true — God wanted me to marry you." ■ "It was the Devil, María. You remember the day you came to our house selling those meringues you make?

Ana Julia and I watched you hike over the ridge. 'I want that woman,' I said. 'Her daddy has land and a house in the village. That's a woman who knows how to make money.'" ■ He smiled and lit a Pielroja cigarette. "All the Vásquez women know how to cast spells. So while you were climbing up to the house, Ana Julia fixed a potion and mixed it with *guarapo*. When you got to the house she handed you the home brew knowing you'd be thirsty. You remember? And then I asked you to marry me. You should be grateful because I could've just carried you off." ■ Mama said he laughed and laughed till he started choking, but I don't believe her. She said she felt like a glass had suddenly broken in her hands, but she refused to leave him, because she knew how people talked about my Uncle Luis — how he'd come limping back home to live with his parents. She said if she had to go, she'd go far away. ■ She worked and tried to keep the household organized. She got up at five, she made breakfast, she ground the corn and fried the meat. When there wasn't coffee to pick, Papa cleared the fields or picked corn. At lunchtime she climbed the mountain to where he was working and served his meal. She loaded the donkeys with the meat, sugar, rice, manioc, pots, plates, everything. When it rained, the slope was treacherous. She was a strong plump woman when she got married but in less than three months Grandmother said she looked like a stick. ■ Papa worked hard but he was a drinker and a brawler. He ended up in jail. Blind Ana told me that what happened was, Papa got drunk and slashed a man with his machete. They sentenced him to two years in El Bordo, a half-day ride away. The day they were to let him out, he got into a little trouble, some kind of jam, God knows what: he wound up killing a guard. So from El Bordo, they sent him straight to the big prison in Bogotá. ■ Every penny they had went for lawyers and Mama's trips to the prison in El Bordo. With Papa in jail, my Uncle Elías took charge of the coffee fields and tried to get rid of Mama. When she went into labor with me, she couldn't stand the pain. She was all by herself in the country, eight-months pregnant. Papa was behind bars. She said she wanted to die, and take me, the baby with her. ■ It turned out the priest who married them was an impostor (he had a wife and kids and he was also a thief; he'd run off with the church money). Everyone in the village said they'd better get married again and rebaptise the kids. With the last of her money, Mama went to Popayán and asked the Archbishop to annul the marriage, but he said no. The moment a guy gets dressed in robes, even though he isn't an ordained priest, the sacraments are binding. So Mama and Papa would be married till the day they died. ■ Before Papa left, they let him come to stay with us. He brought Javier a pull toy and a whistle. Me, he brought ribbons — ribbons for my hair, all kinds of colors. I was very happy just to know he was still alive. ■ Papa must be a giant, I thought, because his head brushed the top of the door. He had blondish hair like me and a long mustache blonder than his hair. His teeth were pretty and white. He was thinner than most of the other men in El Valle. He wore a poncho over his shoulders and carried a machete on his belt and when we walked together, the tip of his machete touched my shoulder. ■ When Papa sold the first of the coffee crop, he bought a rabbit and onions and corn for *arepas*. He whacked the rabbit on the neck with a broom handle, skinned it, put it in the pot, and sat me and Javier next to him. He took a whole onion with the skin still on it and cooked it over the fire, and we ate it! The skin was crunchy and it stuck in my teeth, but it was delicious.

We followed Papa to Bogotá. Mama wouldn't go back to Grandfather Leónidas' house. She sold the livestock to pay for our plane tickets. Grandfather bought us some blankets and clothes. He cried and told us we'd suffer. When we got to the airport there was no flight, so we had to travel by train. Then the train derailed. The engineer and the boiler man were burnt to a crisp. We stood there by the track from four in the afternoon until four in the morning. Thank God, nothing happened to us, only Mama lost the suitcase with half of her money inside. ■ In Bogotá they gave Papa a choice of serving twelve years in the regular prison or two in Aracuara, which was the penal colony in the Amazon jungle. He chose the colony. If he got out alive, he'd get out alive; if he died, he'd die. ■ They shipped Papa to Aracuara. Twenty-five hundred men lived there in one big hall. The only food was boiled bananas and sugar cane to suck on. The prisoners' job was to clear the jungle, but it grew back almost as fast as they could clear it. When they got work, the guards took them up on the road that the convicts themselves had carved out of a cliff and shot them in the head. ■ Papa was made without a single ounce of fear. Two years later he was a free man. But who knows now if Papa is alive or dead? Once you go to prison and get out, you have to be sure it doesn't happen again.

I was six when Mama left the mountains and we came to Bogotá. Everything seemed so strange in Bogotá. The houses were very tall and some of them had little signs, like the sign for Andina, which was a beer, and the beers were tall, too. There was a beer called Little Goat, but I never tried it because the smell of the drunks bothered me and the bars smelled of sweat and spit, not like in the shop where they made dresses with very wide skirts out of cloth with tiny little holes, and patent leather shoes that the Bogotá ladies danced in, kicking so hard the shine scuffed off, and where they made umbrellas that were long and thin (an umbrella was a very strange thing — like a magic stick). Mama had an umbrella for the rain because when it rained the streets got terribly slippery, with a lot of mud splashing up on my dress and everything and on the door of the bakery where they had colanders and sieves, which I liked a lot. I liked to watch them sift the flour, watch the flour go by with each shake, see how it fell, wondering why they sift the flour if it's already so fine? It was so strange and lazy and pretty to sit and watch them shake the flour singing along with *boleros* on the radio, singing "If you have a soul, paint me little black angels because souls are angels sleeping. . . ." So strange. Because in the churches, the pretty little angels all were blond with blue eyes, like Saint Rocco, the saint with the oozing wounds and the skinny dog, and Saint Helen with her crown. So many saints, and how we prayed: black bows on the doors of houses where people had died, and my godfather driving by in a hearse with Saint Joseph and the Virgin Mary, and big balloons flying out the back. ■ My first memory of the city is of La Picota, the prison they put Papa in. It was on the feast day of Our Lady of Mercy, the patron saint of prisoners. The prisoners had made toys for their kids. My older brother, Javier, and I went into the room where all the gifts were laid out. I saw a beautiful bonnet, one of those round little hats covered with flowers and a pink ribbon on the sides. A man with a mustache smiled at me and asked me what I wanted. "I'd like the bonnet please, your honor." He put it on my head so the prettiest flowers were in front. I don't remember seeing Papa. Maybe he was the man who gave me the bonnet. ■ We moved from one house to another. In the first house, the owner's name was Rosa. Then there was Señora Irene, Señora Augustina, then Telita, and Ignacia. An old man named Méndez lived at Ignacia's. When he came home at night he would strut and crow like a rooster. ■ Before we moved into a new room, we cleaned the walls and floor. If there was a little window, we cleaned the glass. We waxed the floor. I didn't like those rooms; they were small and dark. Finally I asked, "Mama, why are we in one house one day, and then we have to move the next day?" ■ "We pay money for this room, so they let us live here. Sometimes I don't have enough money and then I have to go look at other rooms in other houses." After Ignacia we went to live with Ubaldina, which was a half-block away. There we had a room in one corner of the patio; there was no second floor. In those days, apart from paintings such as the Sacred Heart, there was something called Gobelins, which were small tapestries with pretty landscapes. They showed the sea, and palm trees, and women in the water; I thought they were so pretty, with the women sitting and holding flowers. ■ But what I remember most was watching Señora Ubaldina make the bed because the mattress was tied with hemp and filled with straw. On the side where her husband put his head she found a whole pack of rats. When I made my bed, I always looked to make sure it was clean.

Javier took me everywhere. We went for walks in the soccer field all by ourselves. We watched the fancy ladies walking in their high heels. Javier gave me his hand and I raised up on tiptoes and took fast little steps. Sometimes I put on Mama's shoes. It was great feeling the heels biting into the mud. There were no sidewalks in the barrio, no sewers. The streets weren't paved, the rain water ran yellow, full of frogs. ■ Javier wore clean shirts and little soldier pants and shoes with laces. He was thin like me, but when he parted his hair on the right he looked just like Mama. He wrote very prettily with a pencil. After he showed his homework to the teacher, he erased the whole thing and did his next lesson on the same page. He didn't want Mama to have to spend money on a new notebook. ■ Javier made a little cart. He hung around the market after school and waited for the high-heeled ladies to finish their shopping. They paid him five cents to deliver their groceries. He also did the marketing for the Three Happy Guys Restaurant. Whenever he spotted a cheap sack of oranges or maybe a box of old mangoes, he bought them for us. All the kids in the market were his friends because he got food for them. Javier let me taste the mangoes, and the rosy apples with slippery pits and the pastry rings shaped like erasers filled with jelly and sugar cream. ■ The market had everything. They had mattresses, they had flowered awnings over the yucca and bananas. On sunny days everything was shiny. There were ladies strolling in woolen shawls and men strutting in straw hats. There was a dwarf who wore a little cap and cape. They called him Little Banana because he was so small and old. Javier got furious when people threw banana peels at him. "Hey, Bananito," they yelled. "Hey, whittle wheeny!" ■ One store sold corn liquor and hog fritters. The owner was old Señor Antonio. Javier called him Mr. Matchstick because at the top of his pale skinny body he had this head of bright red hair. Mr. Matchstick laughed and sipped rum out of gourds. Javier always got a little taste. ■ Then he worked for Don Alberto, who had a horse and cart and went around collecting old paper and cardboard and selling it to Compañía Cartonera de Colombia (the Colombian Cardboard Company). They drove off at four in the morning and came home late. They sorted all the stuff into giant piles — paper, metal, anything they could sell. Javier was in charge of the horse; he had to put away the harness, plus stack all the cardboard they collected. One night he came home all excited, carrying a package wrapped in newspaper, and in the package was a blue-skinned doll the size of my finger. You could move its legs. I said, "Oh, how lovely, Javier. Thank you. God bless you, Javier." ■ Probably he found the doll in the garbage, but it was very clean. I got some scraps of material from Mama and dressed her up. I kept her tucked in my sleeve, so I could pull her out and play with her when I was working. But why blue skin, I wondered? ■ I made friends with Cecilia, a little girl who lived there too. We collected old sardine tins and rotten potatoes. We played house and Javier was the papa. "I'll peel the potatoes," one of us would say. ■ I waited for Cecilia one afternoon on the patio and when she didn't come, I cried. One of the women who came to clean the house held me over the coffin for a long time. I thought Cecilia was asleep. She had cotton sticking out of her nose, which looked disgusting, but I was too embarrassed to ask someone to please take the cotton out. I wanted to play with Cecilia, but they wouldn't take her out of the box. ■ Javier told me that Cecilia had turned into an angel and all those people would take her to the cemetery and watch her fly away. Now I have an angel friend, I thought, and she is in the sky. I wanted to die so I could find Cecilia.

When Papa got out of the colony he came to live with us again, but he never stayed out of jail for long. Mama said Papa could never escape from the devil squatting in his soul. She said that if I could peek inside him, I would see a red spot with a tiny black dot in the middle. This red spot with the tiny black dot could kill animals, shrivel corn, and cause harm to other people. I had a red spot too, Mama said, and I had to take care to stay away from Papa. Our twin devils could leave our bodies and travel together. ■ I didn't tell Mama I was glad to be like Papa or that every chance I got I looked for him. When we were alone, I watched for his spot to go flying through the air. I imagined it would come out of his mouth and that it was quite big. ■ Mama got pregnant again. When she was about to give birth, Papa sent us out to buy a bottle of rubbing alcohol. In the morning Javier woke me up and took me to Mama's bed. It was dark, but I made out a long white shape at Mama's side. We gathered up all the old clothes we could find and washed them to make diapers for the baby. ■ Six days after the baby was born, Mama handed us the bucket with Papa's lunch in it. He was working in a quarry. She warned us not to sit down in the pit with him, that children had been buried alive by mud slides. ■ Papa waved us towards him. He was in the pit breaking rocks. "Here, come sit down here out of the sun." He gave us some of his soup and a sip of his drink. He didn't say a word. When we finished all the food, he hugged us so close that I could feel his tears on my neck. Then he handed the bucket back to Javier and we left. The next morning when we woke up Papa wasn't there. ■ The baby caught pneumonia. Mama brought him to a hospital but they wouldn't take him in. She pawned her sewing machine to pay for a doctor, but the baby died in her arms on a street corner near the hospital. ■ Mama tore up all the pictures of Papa except one that Javier kept — the one of Papa holding us on the steps of a church. But Mama made Javier take the scissors and snip him out of the picture. The only thing left was his arms around our waists. ■ I was in the first grade in a school called Panamá in the barrio San

Fernando in south Bogotá, but I never finished because that was the year we started running away from Papa. ■ After the baby died, Mama said Papa sent her newspaper clippings about husbands killing their wives when they found them with other men. He said in his letter that the child who died wasn't his. ■ Mama wrote him that she wouldn't live with him anymore. One day, through the window, I saw him outside. Mama told the others in the house to say she'd gone away the day before. He came back with the cops. They came in and said her husband wanted her back. "It's better to patch things up," they said. "You have kids." ■ Mama put on a blue dress — a tailored suit, really — and new shoes, to impress the cops, she said, but I thought she looked stupid. She dressed us and we walked a half-block with the cops. Papa passed them some money, and they left us there in the middle of the street. ■ Papa suggested we go to a café. Did we want something to drink? "We don't have to go anywhere," Mama said. "I'm not going to live with you one more day. I work to make money, you come to take the money. I don't care if you took me to the altar or to hell." ■ For fifteen days we stayed together in his room. Javier said Papa had three knives — one big, one medium and one small — and he laid them across the top of Mama's sewing machine. Papa begged. He cried. He knelt down and swore that he was a good person, that he loved Mama. It was true he had bewitched her to get her to marry him, but he loved her. Please would we forgive him? ■ Papa believed that when you get married, you have to respect the marriage bond to the grave. The way he felt, he couldn't let his children be tossed out into the world, and he couldn't allow his wife to live, because she was unfaithful. He wanted to kill us to break what he thought was a chain of suffering. ■ "Your father is here," Mama yelled to us one Sunday after mass. "But don't go outside, Alicia." ■ I was thrilled. I ran to the window and stood on tiptoes. I saw him dressed like a farmer, in khaki clothes and a wide-brimmed hat, getting off his horse. He picked me up and kissed me on the forehead. "Get your things ready," he said. "We're leaving." ■ I stayed outside with Papa while Mama went back into the house to clean our room. He lifted me up onto his horse and climbed up behind me. I looked at our concrete house with its tin roof. ■ Mama came out with Javier; Papa told me to jump down and get in the horse cart, but Mama pulled me away. ■ "When I tell you to, Alicia, we're going to jump. You grab Javier; there'll be a car waiting for us. You run with him and get into the car." ■ Oh, I was so disappointed. I wanted to tell Papa, but I couldn't. ■ We went to live with Señora Augustina. Papa found us and watched the house. We were living like animals in a cage. We couldn't talk to anyone; I had to sneak out to buy food. I was tired of watching Mama's games. If Mama had a husband, I couldn't understand why she didn't want to live with him. ■ Finally we escaped in a dump truck. But Papa kept turning up. So Mama decided the only way she could lose him was to go back to El Valle. ■ The bus to El Valle was called Magdalena. Mama sobbed at the station because she didn't want to leave. But I was happy we were going to the country. ■ Papa followed us to El Valle; we traveled on one ridge and he traveled on the other. We crossed each others' paths, but we never met. When we got to El Valle, Mama's family said he'd been there looking to kill us. From then on, the worst threat we ever heard was, "Your father is outside." But we never saw Papa again.

I always thought Mama was pretty. She wasn't thin, she wasn't fat. She had long, painted nails and beautiful braids. She wore wide, slightly gathered skirts, and blouses with square necklines. I don't remember her shoes very well. I liked to watch her brush her hair. She'd pick the strands out of the comb and throw them on the floor, so when I swept, the hair would be there. She didn't use make-up. Her skin was pretty and very clear and she had a beauty mark high on her cheek. Other women painted beauty marks on their faces. I'd say: Mama is so rich she doesn't have to paint her beauty mark on. ■ When Papa left and the baby died of pneumonia, Mama suffered so much I thought she was going to die. She got thinner and thinner till her clothes were hanging off her. ■ When her sadness over the baby's death passed, she began to fix herself up. She wore dresses instead of skirts and blouses. She cut off her braids and gave herself a perm. When she sewed at her machine she kept a little bottle of rum next to her. ■ We went to live at Señor Suárez's house. He had chicken coops, and the old man himself had bulgy rooster eyes. That's when Rosalba came to stay with us. She was a friend of Mama's and she worked as a maid. She wasn't very pretty, but she painted herself up and wore fancy, tight clothes. She had a lot of friends who were mechanics. One of the guys was called Rat and he had a son called Rat, too. We felt sorry for the little boy because he was so shy and his clothes were always torn and dirty. Whenever anyone gave us money for bread, we shared it with him. Rosalba walked around the house without a blouse on, and she'd bring the mechanics in the house and send us out to buy bread. ■ One evening Mama left wearing her new pink flowered dress. She stayed away for days. When she came back the pink flowers looked brown, her collar was torn, there were bruises on her arms and her eyes were black. We cried when we saw her. ■ Mama started going out every night. When Rosalba wasn't there, she'd leave us locked in the house.

Whatever happiness Mama had with a man, she said she had with Raúl. She appreciated him. The trouble was, he knew it. She met him at a party in the plaza at Tunjuelito, where they have a bullring and little houses for dancing. She sewed all day and at night she went to the dance with a friend and her husband. Everybody was dancing in the canteen. She noticed a guy who reminded her of the photographer in El Bordo who took a picture of her when she was a girl so Grandfather could send it to the invisible doctors in Mexico to diagnose her chest pains. She said she could tell he was a dancer by the way he moved his body to operate the big camera. ■ The guy sat down at a table outside with three men. He was very well turned out for a peasant. She couldn't keep her eyes off him. He came into the canteen to buy another round of beer for his buddies. ■ "Four more over here!" he shouted. "Speed it up. What's the matter? Your old lady ride you too hard last night?" He grinned and pulled a fifty-peso note out of his pocket. When he looked up, he saw Mama watching him, and he looked back for a long time. Finally he came to Mama's table and introduced himself as Raúl Casas, a young bachelor from Bogotá. He asked if he and his friends could join them. They all sat together and he asked Mama to dance. He said he was single, that his parents had been killed in *La Violencia*, the bloody civil war between the Liberals and the Conservatives. He didn't have a father or mother, no brothers and sisters — nobody. ■ Raúl was a great dancer, and Mama loved to dance. I guess they were crazy about each other — love at first sight, as they say. It went all right in the beginning. Raúl worked as a stone mason, he gave us money for food; and Mama worked, so we lived well. ■ Then people began to ask him why he had hooked up with a woman with kids when there were so many free women around. He thought about it. Then they had a kid of their own. That was an even bigger mistake. ■ From the moment my stepfather Raúl appeared I began to rebel. His clothes didn't fit right. Since Mama was a seamstress, we were always looking at the style and fit of people's clothes. I said to Javier, "This guy that comes to see Mama is so ugly; why does she let him hang around?" ■ Mama said, "Alicia, say hello to your father." ■ "My father? Is my father here?" I looked up at the ceiling. "The man in this room isn't my father. Why should I say hello to him?" ■ Raúl said, "I would like to win the affection of these kids, María. They are little angels." This became his name for us, and I began to hate the word — "*angeleetaaaa, angeleetoooo.*" ■ "Javier," I whispered, "are you a little angel, huh? No! You are walking on the ground. You are Javier and I am Alicia." ■ So my stepfather started to hate me, and I hated him. I hated his picture, the one Mama hung up like it was the most important thing in the world. Raúl looked about nineteen in this picture, with wavy hair, and I hated the stupid spotty suit he was wearing. I hated the radio when he turned it on. I hated the music he liked. He brought home a trophy from a checker championship. I hated his trophy. ■ He started coming home drunk at one or two in the morning and he'd make us get up and wash with ice-cold water while he whipped Mama. He also hit Javier a lot. He'd send him out to get fried fish at all hours of night; sometimes he just kicked him out on the street, and Javier would have to sleep in a gas station. Javier got to know all the attendants. ■ I used to braid my hair with scraps of Mama's ribbons. I'd pass by the mirror quickly because I was afraid. I didn't like looking in the mirror; I was very thin. I combed my hair with my eyes closed. ■ I liked to look at myself in the water, though. I'd lean over the sink and instead of walls I saw the ceiling and I looked at myself and looked at the ceiling and the things that happened around me as if everything was a painting. In the washroom I put my face in the water and made bubbles. I loved to slosh my hands and watch the drops fall. ■ And the rain, it was so pretty to watch. I used to sit on one side of the door and watch the puddles move. Since we lived in Tunjuelito and the streets weren't paved, the water ran yellow. I watched the clean rain fall, and listened to the sound. . . watching it run. When I got depressed or sad, or after Mama hit me, I'd go to the bathroom and stand under the water. The water falling on me made me happy. It was freedom. ■ Mama had a chair with a back made of strips of wood with the bark still on them. Sometimes instead of beating me, she tied me to that chair. She tied my hands around my back; she tied my ankles to the bottom of the chair so that my legs were twisted under me. She left me there for hours and I fell asleep and dreamed. ■ I dreamed I was at school — at boarding school — and it was wonderful. Mama couldn't look at me and I didn't have to look at her. I learned how to embroider beautiful things. ■ I wondered why Mama did this to me. Did they tie her in a chair when she was little? ■ I'd read books about people who were condemned to the gas chamber or the electric chair. What would an electric chair be like? They'd taught us at school that electricity didn't travel through wood, so the seat would have to be made of metal, I decided. And gas? That made me laugh out loud. I couldn't imagine a gas chair. ■ What was it like for those poor men like Papa who were in prison, or the ones that died in prison? ■ I looked around. If only the walls of this house were made of glass, so the sun could shine in. I couldn't stop looking. I couldn't get comfortable. She'd tied my hands so I couldn't scratch my nose. If I could just twist my braids around my neck, I could hang myself. It's a sin, Alicia, so stop thinking about it. Okay, then I'll think about something else. If the walls were glass, I could plant green plants on all sides and see the green, green, green. But the walls are horrible. It's so dark. ■ When Mama untied me at night, I was bent over like something you take out of a box. ■ I escaped to the bathroom and stayed there for hours. I took off my clothes and got into the concrete trough we washed in. I put my head under the cold water and turned the faucet so the water ran harder. The cold made my head ache, but the water seemed to cleanse me inside and out. ■ "Alicia, have you died in the bath?" I made the water run harder. "Alicia!" Not even the water could save me from Mama's voice.

When we lived in Señora Irene's and Don Leonel's house, our room had a door facing the street. The house had wooden stairs that made a nice noise when I danced on them. Behind the house there were fields of peach trees. We ate more peaches than anything else in those days. I used to whack them off the trees with a rope. ■ A little servant girl lived upstairs. Señora Irene had brought her from the country. I wanted to show her that I was her friend, but I never got the chance to talk with her. Señora Irene and Don Leonel beat her if she didn't work fast enough. One day her mama and papa came and got her. I was hoping they would keep her. But six days later she came trudging back. She walked upstairs and disappeared into her room. Just as I started to leave, she opened the door and said, "Come quickly." Her arms were full of fruit. I spread out my skirt to catch it. I said, "Thank you," and asked her name, but when I looked up again she was gone. ■ Most of the girls I knew worked. The way it usually happened was, a girl in the barrio would suddenly disappear, and I would ask Mama, "Where is the daughter of Señora So-and-So? Where did she go?" ■ "They sent her out to board," Mama would say. ■ These girls were very little, like me, so it was not so strange for me to think about it. As soon as they came home for vacation, I was at their houses asking a thousand questions. I didn't leave home till I was seven. It started when a lady asked Mama to make a dress for her. I was taking care of a neighbor's baby when she arrived. "Miss María," she said, "you wouldn't happen to know of a girl whose parents would let her take care of my child?" ■ Mama said she didn't know but she'd ask around. After supper, she said, "Alicia, how would you like to go with Doña Cecilia, to take care of her baby? She's a teacher. But you've got to be very careful not to give the Eye to the baby. You must do the cures." ■ I had trained myself to keep my eyes on the floor whenever I was around a very young child. If I couldn't do that, I'd touch the babies. Sometimes I'd have to slap them lightly so they'd cry. Because when the child cried, that would break my energy; I'd get confused and my eyes would lose their power. ■ The next morning

I packed my blue dress, my stockings, a pair of shoes, toothpaste, a comb, a towel and underpants in a cardboard box. I didn't have deodorant or anything fancy like that. I wasn't afraid; I was filled with curiosity to know what other houses were like. ■ The teacher lady lived a long way from Mama's house. I remember walking with my box tied around my shoulders to the school, where Mama left me. ■ Whenever I arrived at a new house, I felt ashamed in front of the family and their friends. I had to look very neat and wear shoes and socks everyday because the people in these neighborhoods were rich. ■ Mama warned me that I should keep quiet and never talk about anyone. When people got angry, I should be very careful because I was a stranger in their house. If someone spoke to me, I answered "Yes, Ma'am" or "No, Ma'am" and looked at the floor. I mean, I was in their house and they were educated people. ■ I was taking care of children that to my thinking were no longer children. I was always having to dress "little Ricardo" or "little Luis," and these were kids much bigger than me. What I was most afraid of was that they would ask me a question about their homework and I wouldn't know the answer. But it was good to know that I could take care of someone and to realize how dependent these children were. ■ I earned about fifty pesos a month. Mama kept the money to buy shoes or material for a dress. "You should be happy," she said, "that you can buy these things with the money you earned." ■ And I was, but whenever the girl next door saw me, she pulled my hair and shouted so everyone around could hear, "Look, this girl is a servant. I don't do that. I study, and in the best school." ■ I worked on the outside as a servant from when I was seven until I was eleven. I worked for the teacher lady (who was nice), for a secretary, for a druggist who beat me, for a woman who was a friend of Mama's, and for a cripple lady. About six families in all. ■ I liked the teacher's house because we were all equal there. Sometimes, in the other houses, they'd give me only a little scrap of meat to eat, or nothing at all. At the teacher's house, we all ate the same things. ■ One Sunday we went to a restaurant. I'd never seen a place so beautiful. The walls were wood halfway up, the tables were made of glass, the floor was shiny linoleum, and the dishes had drawings of leaves on them; half a leaf was blue and the other was a bleeding color. I liked the clatter of the pretty dishes and the glasses with gold rims. ■ How much money would a person spend here? If someone ate in a restaurant everyday, he'd get so fat he couldn't sit down. ■ We sat down at one of the glass tables. Under it, I could see my red skirt and black rubber shoes. The teacher's husband asked me what I'd like to eat. ■ "Rice and potatoes?" ■ The teacher laughed. "No, Alicia. You don't eat the same here as you do in your house. You can ask for anything you like." ■ So they all ordered different kinds of meat, rice, and vegetables. But I was so terrified I couldn't think what to ask for. ■ "Okay, Alicia will have the fried steak," the teacher told the waiter. "One of the big plates." He brought the biggest piece of meat I'd ever seen. They had such a nice way of flavoring things. ■ I wanted to learn to cook the things we ate at the restaurant because they were so delicious. I didn't realize Mama never had money to buy anything except rice and potatoes.

The cripple lady I worked for could only make tiny movements, but she could talk. She lay in bed all day, propped up by cushions, and surrounded with pictures of saints lit by little candles. She kept her money right underneath her, in the bed. ■ The coins were warm from the heat of her body, but her hands were frigid like the hands of a dead person. Her eyes were always fixed on me to see what I would do next. ■ One day, she threw away some plants in rusty cans. I picked them out of the garbage and put them in bigger pots. In two months they were big and beautiful. ■ The cripple lady didn't like this. She managed to put a picture of the Devil in the tallest of my plants. Then she asked the neighbors if they'd like to see some plants grown by the Devil. "Watch out for the girl with the plants because she has a pact with Satan," everyone was saying. ■ That was the first time anyone called me a witch. I was eleven years old and my first diabolical deed was to resurrect those dead plants.

My stepfather Raúl thought there was something strange about my eyes, even though Mama never told him about the Evil Eye running in the family. When he was drunk, he'd grab me and say, "I know you — you're an evil little girl. You're a monster!" ■ He came into the kitchen while I was cooking supper. He dropped onto the cot in front of the stove. He pulled up the little wooden bench and I sat down. "Look at me, Alicia." I looked at him and kept looking at him and then the tears started running down his cheeks, and more tears. He shouted for Mama. ■ "Look at this! This girl has wicked eyes." ■ "Whose fault is that?" They began to scream and shout like crazy people.

I was eleven when my brother, Miguel Angel Vásquez de Casas, was born. He had black curly hair and he didn't look anything like my stepfather. We called my brother Miguelito. I was careful not to make him sick. I loved him very much. Mama had taught me to look at the floor if a child was nearby. If by mistake I did, I had to do the cures — burn a strand of my hair and put it in the child's bellybutton or pray and make a sign of the cross with my saliva on his neck. Every day I took care of Miguelito while my mother made breakfast and sent Javier off to work. When he was still asleep, I laid out his clothes and when he opened his eyes I was already making the sign of the cross on his neck. What a burden that was. In the end the Evil Eye was really my salvation. I had to look for my own way out, to get away from what others planned for me.

When Mama's customers came around, they ordered very tight things. They wore a lot of prints, the silks were so pretty. They wore long stockings and shawls with tassels. What fascinated me most was the smell of their nail polish: like butter cooked with salt. I wanted to touch, to smell, to feel everything. ■ When I was twelve or thirteen I got very angry at one of the women, Inez, who rented a room next to ours.

She was young and pretty and she worked as a prostitute in a rough place. I knew it was rough because Mama worried about her. One day Inez came home with silver earrings. She grabbed Mama. ■ "María, I'm so happy! Look at these earrings my boyfriend gave me." I jumped up behind Mama to look, but Inez said, "Go away, Alicia. I'm showing these earrings to your Mama." ■ I'd never seen anything made of silver. "What was so special about it that I couldn't look?" I asked Javier. ■ "Are you stupid? Silver is the money we use to buy things with." ■ "No, this is the silver they use for earrings. Women don't hang silver coins from their ears." ■ "It's the color of the electric wires." ■ "Why is it so valuable?" ■ "I don't know, Alicia. Go away. I don't want Mama to see us talking." ■ Mama sent me to the store to buy bread and coffee. So I asked the old storekeeper. "Listen, mister, do you know what color silver is?" ■ "Silver coins?" ■ "No, mister, the kind they make earrings with." ■ "What an inquisitive little girl you are." He smiled and held out his hand. "Look, this ring I'm wearing is silver." ■ "It just looks like a piece of tubing to me." ■ "This is silver. This costs a whole lot of money." ■ "And with this they make earrings too?" ■ "Yes, they make necklaces and earrings for women. What do you want to buy? Or did you come here just to discuss jewelry?" ■ I shoved the money across the counter, picked up my things and ran out. ■ The closer I got to home, the angrier I got. Silver wasn't so special after all. So why didn't this woman want to show me her earrings? I pictured her with big silver strips hanging from her ears chatting with Mama. And then in my mind I watched them drop out of her ears. ■ That night Inez came home and announced that she and her boyfriend were going to get married. She'd just bought some white material and she wanted Mama to make her a wedding dress. She smiled and talked with Mama all evening, but the next night she came in without saying a word. ■ When Inez woke up the next morning, her eyes were swollen. She went straight to Mama, who was lying down. I stood listening in the doorway. Inez was crying. ■ "Oh, María, something awful has happened to me." ■ What happened to this one, I wondered. She's still alive. I had forgotten about the earrings. ■ "This world is finished for me." ■ Mama sat Inez down on the bed. "Calm down. God is in his heaven and as long as you don't lose faith, you won't lack for anything in the world." ■ I was dying of envy. Mama never talked to me so sweetly. "Now, my daughter, tell me what happened." ■ "My daughter — ha!" I wanted to shout at her, "*I* am your daughter!" ■ Inez stopped crying. "Oh, María, would you believe that the earrings Demian gave me got stolen?" ■ I put my hand over my mouth to cover the big grin on my face. ■ I remembered my grandfather: when Marco Tulio couldn't have the things he wanted, he destroyed them. "Ay, Papa Marco Tulio," I prayed, "let something awful happen because they're being so selfish." They taught us in the church not to desire things, but I kept thinking, what is survival but wanting things, to want to live?

Inez decided to leave soon after the earrings disappeared. The day she came to pick up her things, Mama was sweeping outside. When she turned around to look, she saw a familiar face. It was Matilda, who used to live in one of the houses with Papa and us. They chatted a while and then she asked if Mama had been to Papa's funeral. ■ "It was about eight years ago," she said. "They killed him in a bar just past the Tunjuelito River. It was in the newspaper with a picture. I kept it for you." ■ Papa was already drunk when he got to the bar, Matilda told Mama. The barkeep was a dark thin man, a Peruvian named Skinny. Papa drank three more beers. He got into an argument with this Skinny about fifty centavos he thought was coming to him. The Peruvian said he'd already given it to him. Papa told him to step outside. Then he gouged a hole in the counter with his biggest knife and stumbled out to the street, Matilda said. ■ The customers got scared and wouldn't let Skinny leave. Papa heaved rocks through the windows and kept shouting "Hey, dinky dick! Hey, scarecrow!" and kicking the door. ■ Finally Skinny came out behind a switchblade. Papa was a good fighter, but when he threw a punch the Peruvian ducked and Papa fell flat on his face, he was so drunk. Papa stood up and punched him again. Now they were in the middle of the street. Papa belted him again so hard they thought he was dead. But Skinny got up and when Papa came at him, Skinny opened the blade into his chest. Papa staggered and fell dead. Matilda said he didn't have a chance to say a word. ■ Mama told us she'd check the story. Javier said what for? I wanted to know, so Mama went to Tunjuelito anyway and they said yes, they'd had him in the morgue there years ago. Nobody'd claimed him, so they'd buried him in a common grave. ■ Matilda told Mama they'd put a cross with Papa's name on it in front of the bar. We never saw it because one terrible winter the river flooded and washed away three crosses on that spot. Matilda gave Mama her address and told her to come by to see the newspaper. Before we got there, there was a leak in the roof over where she kept her old papers. Her daughters had thrown out the damp paper. ■ Then one day, after Mama had talked to Matilda, Javier was standing in a gasoline line. He asked somebody to mind his place while he went across the street to buy a soda. Then he heard, "Javier, come here." He recognized the voice and turned. He swore it was Papa. Javier ran and hid at the back of the gasoline line.

Our landlady was a little old lady who drank a lot. Her real name was Concepción de Granados but we all called her Conchita. She called Miguelito Wheat Roll because he was fat and brown. On Fridays she went out drinking with all the men who lived in the house. When they got home at dawn, they helped Conchita climb the stairs to her room. Then they went home to fight with their women. ■ Nine of us families lived downstairs and Conchita lived on the second floor. The room we rented was tiny — ten by nine feet — but we squeezed in two beds, a little table, a chair, and Mama's sewing machine. Our only decoration was a mirror used by the women who came to be fitted for their dresses, and a picture of Our Lady of Mount Carmel. ■ The house was ugly. Conchita wanted the floor waxed and shined but you couldn't, it was too rotten. The walls were so damp that if you put the bed next to the wall the mattress would turn moldy. We each had one day to wash. No one else could wash even a sock that day. There was one bathroom for all of us. ■ Some of the people were good. Some weren't. Some left the bathroom dirty and blamed the others. Some stole clothes or food and dumped their garbage in other people's rooms. One girl, Luz Elena, stole underwear, pots, and spoons. She was unpleasant. ■ When Raúl came home drunk, he'd turn up the radio loud. The neighbors would start insulting us and shouting at Raúl to turn it off and let them sleep. Conchita de Granados would have to get up and quiet everyone down. ■ One time Raúl got into it with a guy next door. This guy worked. I don't know where he worked, but he left early every morning and came back after dark. He lived just on the other side of the wall from us. And like always Raúl came home and turned up the radio and woke everybody up. ■ Well, one night this guy was in a bad mood. He woke up and shouted, "God damn it. Let me sleep." And he went to get Conchita, who tripped and rolled down the stairs drunk. Raúl came out and split the guy's head and it all ended at the police station. We slept through most if it. We finally woke up crying. It was time to move. ■ Mama had heard about a *barrio de invasión*

— a new squatters' settlement, actually — named after the only woman military hero in Colombia's history, Policarpa Salavarrieta. Policarpa had run messages between Bolívar and his men. When she was only twenty-one, the Spaniards captured her. She was handed over to a firing squad and shot in the back — the method used by the Spaniards to execute traitors. "Miserable people!" she shouted to the crowd that gathered to watch her die. "I pity you. How different your lives would be if you knew the price of liberty. But it's not too late: watch and don't forget this lesson. I am a woman and young, but I have more than enough strength to meet my death — and a thousand more." ■ People who didn't have roofs over their heads — and there were hundreds of thousands of them in Bogotá — or people like Mama, who wanted to build something of their own instead of renting a tiny room with no light — organized themselves to invade empty land and build houses out of whatever they could find. You had to do it quickly because in a few hours the police might come to knock down the houses and arrest everybody. Then they elected a government. They built a water system. They stole electricity from the light poles around them. The squatters knew that the longer they stayed and the more permanent the structure they could make, the more chance they had of hanging on. The law said the police had thirty days to remove them if they didn't have the right papers, but even then the police could take it up with the judge and get a new order to kick them out. ■ People resisted; some people were killed. Sometimes people from other barrios came to help. They'd make a human chain around the land to keep the police out. (It was hard. The police destroyed lots of *invasiones*.) Gradually the city government had to accept them. Where else were all these people going to live? ■ Mama thought she'd take a chance and invade a new section of Policarpa along with forty new families. We might lose everything, but at least we'd try. We'd just gotten everything together when a neighbor asked Mama if she knew the organizers were communists. She said no. ■ We were raised Catholic. Even to say the word "communism" was a sin. Mama went to the priest and confessed that she'd committed the mortal sin of wanting to live in a communist barrio. The priest said she must not do that, not for all the money in the world, and that a person who was baptised Catholic had to follow the teachings of the church, that she should run away from communism like Satan runs away from the cross, that communism was Satan himself. She was convinced. She said she didn't want to jump into the flames of Hell. We were doing fine on our own; why should we get involved with communists? Then even God wouldn't touch us. But the rents kept going up and everything got more expensive. Mama started working harder, sleeping two or three hours a night. When she got even more work, she took pills to keep her awake around the clock. She got so hooked that when we finally did move to Policarpa, she couldn't sleep right for four years. ■ We were still living in Conchita's house when a traveling salesman rented a room there. He was from the south from near our valley so we got on fine. He invited us out for Christmas Eve and we all had a great time. The salesman mentioned he'd joined an organization called Provivienda and they were going to assign him a parcel of land in a new barrio in Policarpa. He was going to invade next week. Why didn't we join up too? Mama told him that frankly she was afraid. "Are the organizers communists?" ■ "Of course, they're communists. The communists are the ones who help the people. But they don't force you to become a communist if you don't want to be one." ■ He was a good and honest man and Mama says she always pays attention to honest people. But still she couldn't go. She said she felt like a hand was holding her back. The salesman insisted that we visit him in the Charles de Gaulle barrio, which was named for the day they invaded it, the twentieth of July, the day de Gaulle arrived in Colombia. Mama made excuses; she lied. She told him she was very sick. ■ "Look, María," he said, "one day they'll throw you out on the street, and then you'll have to deal with the situation yourself because I'm not going to beg you anymore. If you're tough enough to work twenty-four hours a day, what's so hard about making a home of your own?" ■ Then, just like the salesman predicted, our situation got worse. Javier lost his job. Conchita de Granados raised our rent fifty pesos, which was a lot of money then. So Mama joined Provivienda, the squatter's organization, along with some other women. Now that Raúl didn't always come home, she made her own decisions. After the last Provivienda meeting before the scheduled invasion,

Conchita de Granados evicted us. ■ The other squatters said they'd get the wood for our new house. Just bring an old bed and mattress, they said. ■ We moved into the community center built by the first group of squatters in Policarpa. (Five years earlier they had invaded the empty fields around Hortua Hospital, where later the government said it had planned to build a new hospital.) All those families in one building, baby bottles all over the place, common meals cooked in enormous pots — people started getting sick. They trucked in milk and groceries and we had to stand guard and when the doctors came from Hortua Hospital they said we had to build real houses or there'd be an epidemic. ■ It was Good Friday in 1966. The shacks were all made with sticks and paper and cloth. We set up poles for the sides; we had tarpaper for the walls and tin for the roof. Each house was a black box you put beds in. Javier wrote our name in crayon on each board, so when everything was unloaded we'd know where it belonged. ■ At noon, just as we were about to eat lunch, the organizers gave the order to invade the field in front of the hospital. They had already torn down the fence around it. Some of us went over the Hortua Hospital wall, and the others got in through the farm next door. We didn't all go in at one time, just a few through here, a few through there. I was so scared I walked like I was on stilts. ■ Raúl and some of his friends put their shoulders under the corners of the black box and raised it carefully. Now our black box had legs. Everyone ran into the field, carrying the house frames and setting them down in blocks. When Mama and I got there, Javier, Raúl, and a gentleman named Luis Alberto Vega had set up our house and the things were already inside. Luis Alberto Vega was not a leader or anything, just a sympathizer. He got killed on Easter Sunday, the day of the battle. ■ They set the shack down on a floor of grass, like a green carpet. Our little shack made the dirt into a beautiful rug. When you wanted to open the door or let the sun in, you rolled the tarpaper around a stick and threw it on the roof. Then you had a bright house without windows or anything. So in fifteen minutes it was done.

By one-thirty on Easter Sunday, when the police showed up, we were ready. Protestors and help arrived from everywhere. The organizers gave orders for the women and children not to leave. I lit a fire and boiled water to throw at the police. ■ The president of Colombia, Guillermo León Valencia, who was so unpopular he had to declare a state of siege to keep himself in power, watched the gun battle from the terrace of the hospital. ■ The army surrounded the barrio. They made holes in the wall around the hospital to let the cavalry in. The soldiers were shivering from the cold. The rice and flour merchants brought trucks full of food and blankets for the squatters. The police wouldn't let them through. But when the shift changed, the new soldiers were careless. The trucks drove right through the holes in the hospital wall. ■ The orders were that if they attacked us, we should throw rocks. ■ Suddenly there was olive green everywhere. The police came and then the cavalry and you could hear shots. The families below us were being beaten and their houses ripped apart. Mama went to help them. Javier was on the hill waving a flag made out of a white sheet and he was helping to carry the rocks the men were throwing at the police. I stayed in the house with Miguelito so nothing would happen to him. ■ "Even if they knock the house down," Mama said, "don't you leave." ■ The bed was set up in the middle of the room. Miguelito was playing in the bed and he reached out to grab a toy from the ground and just then the cavalry galloped by and all of a sudden the point of a bayonet sliced through the tarpaper and just missed his hand. ■ The adults had a supply of rocks ready. As soon as she heard the first shots, Mama got afraid. But she ran ahead anyway, and when that tremendous battle began she said she forgot all about us and everything. The only thing that mattered was to attack because the police were firing at them. Some of the kids were collecting rocks, and there were rocks flying every which way, and they drove the police back twice. ■ It was worse on the opposite end — away from the hospital — where they sent in the cavalry. Everybody had thick branches with very sharp points, and balls of rags, tied together with wire and asphalt and drenched in gasoline. So when the cavalry charged, they lit their torches and poked them under the horses' flanks and the horses threw their riders way up in the air. When the cavalrymen fell, they lost their weapons and ran but the people didn't just stand there looking at them; they kept pelting them with rocks and throwing hot water on them. ■ The police started shooting through the houses. The organizers shouted to the men to leave, so the police could see there were only women and children inside. They shot one man who'd built his house above us and they kicked him and dragged him around in front of us. What finally calmed things down in the end was a rain shower at four in the afternoon. ■ They say we live in the most Catholic country in the world. It was Easter Sunday and every family had an altar in their shack. The goons went in anyway and after the battle the statues of the saints were still there, crushed in the mud by the policemen's horses. ■ They brought in police cars to take away the wounded on both sides. They said none of the policemen died but I myself saw a dead one. They took Luis Alberto Vega to his house because he didn't die immediately. Two children died later, I heard. They took a lot of us to jail. The police said: tell us who brought you here and we'll give you a house to live in. But we were ready for that. We said: it was need that brought us here; we came here because we don't have money to pay rent and the landlords threw our things into the street. The police said we were dirty commies but they let us go. ■ We held Luis Alberto Vega's wake in the community center. They wouldn't let anyone leave to bury the body in a cemetery so we buried him under Twenty-sixth Street. ■ The police had to be careful after that, because word got out that they'd been so cruel.

Those were good times. We were young. Every morning I'd pull back the blanket, trying not to uncover Javier's brown feet next to my head. I stepped out of bed and looked at the picture of Saint Lucy pasted to the headboard. The beautiful saint with brown wavy hair and blue eyes would protect me until I climbed into bed again. I walked quickly, trying not to trip over one of the trenches Mama had dug in the dirt floor. The floor turned into mud when it rained unless, when the shower began, Mama dug a trench to let the water flow down the mountain. ■ We played hide-and-seek in Antonio Nariño school. The playground was tiny.

I learned to draw the map of Colombia. Almost all of us lived in Policarpa, but when we enrolled we had to lie about that. If we said we were living in the squatters' camp, they would say we were bad students and expel us. I used to say that I lived in a barrio way in the north. ■ But we were happy even if the floor was muddy or high grass grew up in our house. It was a wonderful place to play. Since we didn't have water we had to walk three blocks to the public faucets and carry it back in buckets. Mama wanted to build something in brick right away, so she began washing clothes, sewing, doing a thousand things. ■ We took turns standing guard. We had to make sure no strangers came in at night. If anybody saw anything, they called out, and the first one to reach the alarm, rang it. The kids did guard duty, too. We walked and walked and listened to the adults talk about a lot of things. That the women should be more active; that washing and ironing isn't all there is to life. That we should all contribute time to the barrio. That we had to go talk with the government to demand services in the barrio. . . so they'd legalize our status fast. ■ We'd heard a new *invasión* was planned. We understood that housing was very important, and because we already had a place to live we wanted to help others. At three in the morning the leaders went from house to house like an alarm clock. "Sister, do you want to come with us and help our brothers and sisters take their land?" ■ Nuevo Quindío was hilly, and colder than Policarpa. We had to go around the mountain to avoid the police. To sleep we had to dig up the sod in the pasture and wrap ourselves in it. We put the children between two adults so they wouldn't freeze. ■ They caught Javier when he was bringing in food. You could get two to twenty months for invading. They put him in the district jail. They told him we were subversives, but we didn't even know what the word meant. I knew only that my brother was my brother and Mama was Mama. We were raised to go after what we wanted. We learned a lot about justice and injustice. We had proof that to get a piece of land you had to fight for it. No matter what.

There are healers who invoke saints and healers who don't; then there are healers who prescribe herbs or tell their customers to paint their doors with gasoline or light a candle and chant — things like that. Healers handle good and evil, but not the way you handle a machine. What is evil for one person is not evil for another. It depends. . . . Healers use their power to teach us to defend ourselves.

Javier and his buddies had built the first two rooms of our brick house and they'd wired it with electricity stolen from the light box on the corner. Raúl was working — he had a job carving gravestones for a guy. ■ Raúl earned good money, but he'd always avoided his family responsibilities. So Mama said to him, "You ought to do something for your mother instead of just spending your money on beer. Let's bring her to live with us." ■ She was in a bad way. My own mama was always a hard worker but she never had to work so wretchedly hard as Aurora Calderón did. We found her in an irrigation ditch, standing up to her waist in water under the burning sun of Tocaima in the middle of the day, washing clothes for other people so she could buy food and beer. She didn't want to come home; Mama had to persuade her. And this was the woman who ended up trying to take over our family. ■ After a few weeks she insisted Raúl throw Mama out. Then everything went bad. ■ We were sitting around just talking when all of a sudden the light bulbs began to fly all over the place. Mama set her coffee cup on top of the sewing machine, and BAM! the cup split in two. I put some fruit in the blender; the blender blew up. A white cottony fungus started covering the walls of our house; in the morning we found our shoes all white with the stuff. Mama was a good seamstress — if you brought material and said you needed a dress for tomorrow, she'd make the dress — but her customers stopped coming. It was time to send for a doctor to heal the house. ■ Don Juan was a healer who used only his mind. He always had a little book in his hands and he looked directly at the person he was with. He was a nice-looking old man with light-colored eyes, not very tall, just a peasant in a white shirt. ■ He walked all over our house chanting things. Then he stood in the middle of the big room and said, "Everyone in the house step forward, please." ■ Javier and Raúl and Mama and Miguelito and I gathered in the room. Don Juan grabbed Raúl's arm. "Now look," he said, "your mother is a bad person. Look how she's got you all mixed up. If the salt falls on your wife, it will fall on you too. Tell your mother to lay off the witchcraft because Saint Peter is waiting and she'd better be ready. If she can't do any good, at least she shouldn't do evil. You're her son, tell her to stop. These innocent people. . . ," he waved his hand, "are paying a terrible price." ■ In that instant Don Juan taught me how important it is to recognize bad people when they come into your life. ■ Raúl hung his head. He was forever telling us his mother was a saint, and that my mama was sinful for quarreling with her. ■ Don Juan aimed a finger at a box of clothes we'd just ironed and folded. "Señor," he said to Raúl, "you are the son of the woman who's causing all these problems. You pull out what's in there." ■ Raúl pulled out a little bag tied at the top. Inside were coins, medals, and some herbs. ■ "By the blood of the Blessed Virgin!" Mama said. "I look in that box every time I clean and I never found a thing. Children, cross yourselves. This is a punishment straight from God." ■ Each object in that little bag represented a spell. The coins were to curse my family's luck with money and the herbs were poisons to make us sick. The minute they were removed, things began to change. The white fur on the walls dried up and disappeared; Mama started getting orders for dresses again, and my stepfather and Javier found work. Aurora Calderón went to live with one of her daughters.

The winter Josefina came, people were getting sick from the rain that ran from the pastures and carried tiny bugs down the mountain and into the aqueduct. The bugs got into the brains of some of the children and they went into convulsions and died. ■ Josefina had a baby girl who was two months old when I first saw her, big and chubby. She hadn't been baptised yet, so she had no name. She was an angel. She had golden ringlets and her eyes were blue and her little mouth was bright red and her skin was white. I'd never seen a creature so beautiful except in the holy pictures in church. ■ I loved to watch when Josefina dressed her. That's when the trouble started. I forgot to make the sign of the cross on her forehead. So it was my fault. Sometimes I think maybe that's not true, that it was only something Mama said. Maybe it doesn't really matter. But I should have been more careful. ■ The angel baby got thinner and thinner every day. None of my cures or prayers helped. Her hair lost its shine and her eyes went blank. You could see her skeleton through her wrinkled skin. She looked like a little old lady. Josefina was desperate, but I couldn't comfort her or tell her why. ■ I snuck away from Mama every day to see the angel baby. I prayed to God and his Holy Mother that she not suffer anymore, that they take her. The week that she died, I stood next to her crib and couldn't stop crying. The only thing that comforted me was the thought that she died because she was not meant to be in this world; she was too perfect. ■ I began to dream a lot about a red sky. There was a boy with a kite in the dream, and a terrifying but beautiful painting. It was abstract, all in reds. It was framed with a white frame and the painting pulsed in and out, as if it was breathing. ■ I kept my candle lit and stashed extra ones so I could read in the dark. I read the dictionary. I looked up all the words I could think of. I read so many books. Some of them I didn't understand. Every night lasted years. ■ One morning — it was just before my fifteenth birthday — while I was lying in bed, I felt someone enter the room. I opened my eyes and looked at everything and listened to every noise. The only thing was, I couldn't move. Something was hovering over me. I saw a figure of an animal or a stooped old man who was being moved from overhead, like a puppet, and I saw shadows shaped like people, like an audience watching the struggle between the old man and myself, and I wanted to shout for help, but I couldn't and I felt the breathing of my brothers and sisters and I tried to imagine that we had a window in the room and I could see the sun through the curtain, but then the old man was sitting on my chest, crushing me, and I couldn't breathe, and the next thing I remember Mama was jerking me out of the bed and saying, "Stop screaming, Alicia!" ■ I saw the angel baby in her bed, and I saw Papa walking towards me with a little bag of cookies. I tried to touch him, but he passed me by. Mama was shouting at me: I hadn't washed the dishes. She grabbed a coat hanger to swat me. Something inside me exploded. Everything looked white, and I screamed. "It's not my fault, it's not my fault!" ■ Mama whispered my name in such a sweet voice, "Alicia. . . Alicia. . . ," and asked me how long I'd been having nightmares and I said for years, for ages, for centuries. ■ "Then we have to get up early tomorrow, Alicia, to see Don Juan." ■ I trembled. I was terrified of seeing Don Juan again. He could put himself in my thoughts. I had impulsive, malicious thoughts against almost everyone. "When I face that man," I decided, "I will try to keep my mind very still." ■ At four in the morning we took the bus past the airport to Fontibón, where Don Juan lived. Most people came before daylight to get a good spot in line. Inside, the room was white and empty except for Don Juan sitting on a crate. Next to him was a cardboard box that he told people to leave whatever they wanted in. He was wearing a poncho and wool pants and his canvas slippers, and in a shoulder bag he carried his books. He was the heart of simplicity — very relaxed and friendly with everybody. He made jokes and looked around while saying prayers and meditating with the person in front of him. ■ The people who came to him had so many problems — all caused by bad luck, they said. Some were saying prayers over pictures of people they wanted to have cured. Others were explaining that someone had cast a spell on them. Don Juan told the people they had to be loyal to him while they were under his care; they must not go to a medical doctor. If they weren't concentrating, he picked up on it and wagged his finger at them. ■ "This old man has got to be a phony," I said to myself. "How can he perform miracles while he's making jokes?" When my turn came, I walked up to him with my head bowed. ■ "So you think I'm a phony?" ■ I twitched. I couldn't keep my heart still. I wondered what else he knew. ■ "I know you have nightmares, Alicia. You know I can cure you but you still treat me like a faker — right?" ■ I couldn't move my mouth. "Please," I pleaded with my eyes, "don't say anymore because my mama will beat me." ■ Mama was right behind me.

"Señora, come here," he said. "You don't have to beat her so much. She is stubborn and nervous, but her mind isn't evil, it goes towards good." ■ "Yes, Don Juan." I couldn't tell by Mama's tone what she thought of his advice. "Don Juan, my little girl — she has the Evil Eye." ■ "I understand." He looked in my eyes. "Young lady, you made that little girl very sick, didn't you? Don't be ashamed. Many times it's not a person's fault. We inherit powers and we don't know if they're good or bad. Now we have to do something about your eyes. How many children have you affected?" I had lost my voice. My face was hot and I was trembling. I was afraid and I wasn't afraid. ■ "Young lady, stand up so I can look at your eyes." ■ He had kind eyes, playful eyes. I like to look at eyes. Eyes say many things. ■ "Young lady, don't you dare cast your Evil Eye on me." ■ I ducked my head. He was a very good person. He hadn't looked angrily at me. He tucked his hand under my chin and raised my head. ■ "You're a grown-up lady. Why are you still wearing braids?" ■ I just looked at him. Mama answered for me. "She likes braids. She doesn't want to cut her hair yet." ■ "Ah, she looks like a little girl, but she's quite old, isn't she? This girl has something inside her. Alicia, that head of yours, it doesn't have to be stuffed with horrible thoughts." For as long as I could remember, I thought I was bad and there was no way to fix it. Don Juan's soft voice splintered my thinking. ■ "When your mind is thinking about evil," he said, "it will only attract evil. Let's see if we can conquer this idea. At night, if you pray to God, pray for sleep. You have to study. Yes, you have to excel, but you have to rest, too, because if you're tired you can't accomplish the things you want." ■ He sang: "Lord Jesus came to Bethlehem. Evil walked out and goodness walked in. Saint Lucy, Virgin Martyr, by the power God has given you, save these eyes from sin." He waved three leaves over me. He looked at me and then waved them again. "Ready?" he asked with a smile. ■ I tried to take a step towards the door, but I couldn't stand up. ■ "Let the child rest," Don Juan said. "Sit her down here and wait a minute. She has to rest because she's been very unhappy, very disturbed." ■ Mama led me to a wooden box that Don Juan's wife had brought in. He made me sit down where I could feel his gaze. My body was a big weight. I couldn't feel my arms. I couldn't even open my eyes. This strange sensation lasted a half-hour. Then it felt as if something heavy was leaving me. My thoughts were white and tranquil. My mind was free. ■ That night I slept the whole night.

My face was a mass of pimples. I thought if I painted my eyes no one would notice. ■ Javier came home one day with a bag of nail polish, lotions, mascara, eyeliner, eyeshadow, and everything else I could imagine. Some factory had thrown out their old stock and Javier had gone out of his way to collect it. ■ I'd seen women with very beautiful make-up on TV, but I thought it was just for them. When Javier handed me the bag of creams and eye makeup, I mixed them all together. Miguelito said I looked like a clown from the traveling circus, but finally I learned to use the rouge to make my cheeks look pink, and the blue and green shadow to make my eyes look bright. Now people looked at what I wanted them to look at — my eyes. ■ Mama never spoke to me about sex and my friends wouldn't tell me because they thought she'd get mad. I didn't know what it was to be with a man. And it was a year after I got my period before I knew why the blood came every month. ■ I had breasts and I liked to run through the streets with only a thin cotton blouse on. The night before my fifteenth birthday, Mama hired four musicians to serenade me. At midnight they played love songs on the street in front of our house. The music floated into my dreams and woke me up. But later that night, one of the musicians got stabbed to death. ■ Eleven days after, we were invited to a mass in memory of the musician's soul. I'd gotten a watch with a gold band for my birthday, so I told Mama I'd go home after school and leave the watch in my room before going to mass. She told me no, go straight to church. ■ I was supposed to meet her on the chapel steps. I was carrying my books and wearing my new watch. Just as I turned the corner by the bus stop, I felt something tugging on my arm. I looked and saw one of the street kids running away with my watch. I screamed but no one was there to help me. I got the feeling that something really bad was waiting for me. ■ Mama and Javier and Miguelito had gone ahead, so I caught the bus alone and ended up in a barrio that had just been built. I was confused. I didn't see a chapel and no one knew about a mass for a musician. I had only ten centavos in my pocket. It was getting dark. No one was on the street but six men, who were laughing and walking towards me.

I woke up at sunrise, lying in a field in front of an unfinished apartment building. Two sheep were tethered nearby. I was cold. My dress was ripped. I was covered with mud. I saw cars down below me, so I started walking to the street. Finally I found a bus stop. I got on and begged the driver to let me ride even though I didn't have any money. He thought I was one of the street kids and he said, "Okay, get in the back." ■ As soon as I walked in the door, Mama started yelling and waving a metal coat hanger. "Where did you take off to?" ■ I was crying. "But it wasn't my fault, Mama. It wasn't my fault. There were six guys. Mama, I don't know what happened. I don't know who the men were." ■ "How can you go to school? What if you're pregnant? You knew what was happening. You sold yourself to those men." ■ "What does that mean, Mama?" ■ "A whore like you doesn't have the right to raise your voice to me." ■ "Ay, Señora María!" The widow lady Luzmilda came running into the room. "What a disgrace in this house. I am leaving. You can have your room back." ■ Everybody in the barrio had seen me come home that morning. My clothes, my arms, my legs, and even my hair were covered with mud where the guys had rolled me around. I didn't care what people said, so if anybody asked, I told them what happened. One of Mama's friends, Sandra, was always kind to me. She told me what happened. "Those men raped you, Alicia." ■ I took off my torn clothes and vomited and vomited. I got into bed and stayed there for days. From that time on, I had no options in Mama's house. I went to school. I came home. That's all. I finished elementary school that year and they gave me a diploma. I went home with my little paper and I thought that would ease my shame. Mama just yelled. ■ "You tramp. Do you really think you deserve this?" ■ The rape changed my life. Now I wasn't like the other girls.

Raúl got this idea to sell Mama's sewing machine because he wanted to start a business. This time, he said, he meant it; he was going to work hard. ■ I went with Mama to visit a good friend she sewed for and Mama told her what he'd said. ■ "Pardon me for butting in," the friend said, "but I'd like to know what you're using for brains. What on earth are you going to sell your sewing machine for? You think you'll be better off scrubbing toilets or washing clothes than you are sewing? The machine is your livelihood. You're a fine dressmaker. That's what you should be doing." ■ "But my husband needs the money. He's going to start a new business." ■ "You still believe that? It never occurred to me you were so stupid." ■ So then Raúl said he wanted Mama to sell the house and give him half the money because the law says that when a piece of property is sold, even though the man hasn't put one penny into it, he has the same rights to it as the woman. Mama and Raúl had such a bad fight I got scared. He stayed but Mama stopped speaking to him. He might as well have been trying to talk to the kitchen table. They lived together for a year and a half without saying a word to one other. Raúl slept at the bottom of Mama's bed. Finally he left. ■ He came back again and said very seriously that they should get together for the sake of their son, Miguelito. He realized Miguelito must be missing his father. Raúl said he was going to change. ■ "Okay," Mama said, "you're a grown man. I am a grown woman. Tell me the truth: this house, do you consider it yours? Or whose is it?" ■ Raúl made a noise in his throat. ■ Mama continued. "If you think this house is really yours, go to the councilman in the barrio with witnesses and receipts for the building materials and tell him that I don't have any right to be here because I have other children that aren't yours. See, I'm still young. I'm not fifteen years old, but I feel young. My hands are still very strong. I have my children to support me and help me work. The only thing I ask is that you let me take my clothes and the kids' clothes and we'll leave. If you think this house is yours, I'll go. You don't owe me a cent." ■ He bent his head and began to cry. "María, I know this house is yours. You built it and earned the money to buy the brick and tin and you bought the food for us. That's why I got drunk all the time. I was so ashamed that I couldn't help you. What I said to you about the house being mine, I don't really believe that. I only said it to make you stay." ■ "You can't make me stay with you. I won't live with you one more minute. If I can leave my legal husband, I can leave you. This house isn't yours and it isn't mine. It belongs to all the kids because Miguelito has just as much right to it as Julián's kids." ■ He left. It was too late to keep the family together.

I was combing my hair when a guy came out of the cigarette store dressed like a hippie — gaucho pants and sandals and long stringy hair. Not my type. I liked very together guys who wore jackets and clean shirts. This guy is too much, I thought. But maybe I'll just go downstairs and get a better look. ■ He stopped in front of the house. "Good morning," he said. "Who are you?" ■ "What do you mean, who am I? I live here. My mama owns this house." ■ "Really?" The guy stood there looking me up and down. "Small world, isn't it?" ■ I didn't know what he was talking about and I wasn't interested in finding out. He stank of rum. ■ The next day he rented the back room from Mama. It was a mystery who he was, where he came from, and why he was living with us. ■ Helena from next door said, "That monkey has a wife downtown named Gloria and they have three kids. Probably had a fight with his woman and she kicked him out." ■ Fernando pursued me from the moment we met in the doorway. I already had a boyfriend who sold emeralds. I didn't like him very much, but he took me to wonderful dances. He asked Mama if we could get engaged. She said it was all right with her, then he disappeared. But I always talked about how I had a commitment to this guy. ■ That fool Fernando kept bothering me and sending me messages with Señora Myriam. "Tell him I'm engaged to the emerald dealer," I said every time she handed me a new note. ■ Fernando was forever talking things over with Mama. He bought a suit for his birthday, gray wool. He put it on and sat with us in the kitchen. ■ "Even though this is my birthday and I have a new suit," he announced, "I want to tell you my happiness is not complete, María." ■ "Why, Fernando?" Mama asked. ■ "Well, I'm in love with a girl, but she isn't in love with me." ■ "Oh, don't worry. These things take time." ■ He started cleaning his nails with a little knife he always carried. It slipped and cut deep into his left index finger. He started bleeding like crazy. Out of curiosity I got close to look. ■ "Alicia, bring a cloth," Mama said. Alicia, bring this. Alicia, bring that. ■ I went in and out of the room bringing things so she could stitch the cut. The guy was dying with delight, and I began to think he'd cut himself on purpose. "Come on, Mamita, bring me a glass of water," he said. I told him he was a creep. "You drink. I know you have a wife and kids. Do me a favor — don't talk to me and don't bother me." ■ "You just don't appreciate me, little lady. Trust me." ■ "I'd sooner eat string than your lies." ■ I got invited to go dancing. I put on my dance dress and new stockings and panties. Fernando came by and said, "So you really can't stand me, Blondie?" ■ "No, Señor, it's not that I can't stand you; it's just that you are a man with family commitments." ■ "I'm asking you for the last time, Alicia. It's your own heart you're breaking. Some day you and I are going to dance — that's all there is to it." ■ I can't remember exactly when I turned my eyes toward Fernando, but by the next Saturday I'd stopped dancing with other guys. ■ Mama had given me some terrible beatings that week. One night Fernando found me crying and asked me what was going on. He knew Mama hit me a lot, so I told him how discouraged I was. ■ The next day Mama gave me another beating. "If I can just get away from this house. . . ," I said to myself. "If I can just get up the courage to leave. . . ." ■ Fernando and I talked again. He told me about how his mother had left him — abandoned him on the street — and how he'd had to eat food out of garbage cans. After that I felt closer to him than anyone else in the house. The next morning while Mama and I were washing clothes, he showed up again. ■ "Good morning, mother-in-law," he said. ■ "And why do you say that?" ■ "Because of your light-skinned daughter here." ■ "How much you want to bet this woman won't go with you?" ■ "How much you want to bet she will?" ■ Fernando and I started living together in the little room he rented from Mama. I couldn't figure out how it happened: if this guy was such a lush and already married, what was I doing with him?

What illusions I had! I thought I'd already finished the hardest part of my life. Instead I was stuck with a man full of rage and bitterness. ■ I knew Fernando had problems, but he reassured me. We left Mama's house and went to Medellín, a city almost as big as Bogotá, where Fernando's father lived. We had a shop there where we made beautiful furniture. Then we went to live on the coast, to the village of Necoclí, and we opened another shop. I was Fernando's only helper, I worked alongside him in the jungle cutting wood, then sawing it. I had to wash, too, and cook, and clean, and work a full day in the shop. ■ We'd been married seven months when Fernando grabbed all our money and took off with another woman. At first all I did was cry. Then he started bringing women to the house. He said I wasn't his wife — only a maid he'd imported from Medellín. He told his lady friends he felt sorry for me. He was like a clown putting on a performance to see how I'd react, always looking for ways to torture me. ■ When he left the house, he locked me in. There I sat all day long in our little room, always dark, no matter what house or town we lived in. ■ One day, when we were still in Medellín, Fernando's father took me aside and said, "Look, girl, I'd give you the bus fare back to your mother's, but it wouldn't do any good; Fernando put a spell on you." ■ I'm not sure just when I fell into the trap, but it might have been the night I left my clothes out in the kitchen ready to put on for the dance. There was an old man who lived nearby. I was frightened of him because they said he hypnotized children in the neighborhood, so when I passed by his house, I always walked as fast as I could. I think Fernando took my underwear to the old man and he performed some kind of black magic with it. Now I was completely dependent on Fernando.

We had a very big fight. Fernando hit me so hard I got bruised all over, and weak. I sat on the bed and cried because I didn't have the strength to move. ■ I kept vomiting; my body shook from the cold. The next day I felt I'd been born again, like I had left the cave and could go out into the sunlight. ■ But my stomach still wasn't working right. I was washing clothes that morning with a fourteen-year-old girl who lived across from us, and all of a sudden I started shaking and retching. "You know what's happening to you?" she said. "You're pregnant, my friend." ■ I still didn't know how a child was conceived, or how a baby was born. But she was right. Two or three months had passed since I got my period, so I told Fernando I was pregnant.

He got furious. He said the child I was carrying wasn't his. ■ "So what happened?" I asked myself. "How do people get pregnant?" Mother of God, I hated that man more than anything. He took advantage of my ignorance whenever he could. ■ In December, when I was six and a half months pregnant, we returned to Bogotá. Mama could see I wasn't the same old Alicia. Not only was I pregnant, but Fernando bossed me around. ■ Mama took a picture of me to Don Juan and asked if it was possible that someone had done something to me. Don Juan studied the photograph carefully and told Mama to bring me in. ■ Fernando started arguing with me while we were waiting in line at Don Juan's. Don Juan saw what was going on. "Please — the lady who's expecting and the young man — will you kindly come up front?" We made our way up. ■ "Why are you trying to hurt her," Don Juan said, "when she hasn't done a thing?" ■ Fernando blushed. ■ "Ah, so you're one of those men who can't get a woman by decent means. You're a horny guy, too, aren't you? Don't bother lying. A woman should be won decently, by loving means." ■ Fernando kept quiet. Don Juan looked at me and recited some words. Mama had to prop me up, because I felt like two cents. I was shivering, I was angry that everybody was looking at me. ■ I went back to Mama's house. My baby was born. We named him Hernando and I consoled myself by caring for him. Fernando said that the child had taken his woman's love away. Finally he left the house because he knew he could no longer dominate me. ■ I went back again and again to live with him, trying to rebuild my home because it was very hard for me not to have one. But each time I went back, things got worse.

By the baby's first birthday, I was pregnant again. When Fernando found out, he began to think that I was seeing another guy. So he bought a knife — a machete, really — and he marched around slicing the air with it. ■ "Someday I'll catch you with your boyfriend and this knife will be baptised in your ribs." ■ That Saturday night he came home slobbering drunk. He swore that he'd seen some guy climbing out the little kitchen window ten feet above the floor. "You're a w-w-whore," he stuttered, "just like your m-m-mama." ■ I laughed. "Only a pinhead like you could fit though that window, Fernando. Your mother must've been a pervert. A junkie. A whore. Because how else could she bring such a screwed-up son into the world?" ■ He grabbed the machete from under the mattress and yanked my hair. He held the blade to my throat and sawed from side to side. The metal cut my skin. "Say your prayers, Alicia, because now I'm going to kill you." ■ He was shaking. He snatched the pack of cigarettes out of his shirt pocket, lowered the machete, and leaned it against a chair so he could light his cigarette. When he struck the match, I lowered my arm evenly so I wouldn't attract his attention, and I grabbed the handle of the machete. "Dear God," I prayed, "please don't let me kill this guy; I just want to hit him a few times." ■ He didn't notice my hand on the machete. He took a few drags on his cigarette. He threw it down and tried to grab the machete. ■ "Give me that, bitch." He punched me in the stomach. I straightened myself up and whacked him across the shoulders. I held the machete blade up, so I'd only hit him with the dull side. He spun around and I raised my hand again. I started hitting him and hitting him. I lost control. He got down on his knees and begged me to leave him alone. "Forgive me, Alicia, I was only fooling around." ■ "For all the things you have done to me in our life. . . ," I screamed, "for all those things I've been collecting. . . ." And I kept hitting him. I wanted him to know that when you hit somebody it hurts. Fernando was my enemy; I had to destroy him. ■ He shoved me back into the kitchen. The baby was in a little crib I'd made, in the corner by the stove. Fernando pushed me harder and knocked me down. When I fell I held the knife under me so he couldn't get at it. He jumped on top of me and started punching me in the face. He grabbed a sheet and tightened the ends around my neck. When I tried to breathe, my body felt like it was in one place and my head some place else. The light dimmed and everything went blurry. All I saw was Fernando's face. He was making fun of me, laughing. The bells were ringing in the church below. I was dying and the bells were ringing. I wanted to laugh. My head was going to explode and my body was fighting because my blood stopped pumping and the air wasn't getting to my lungs. I was dying. ■ Somehow, I don't know how, I grabbed the clothes iron by the cable and smashed it over his head. I smacked him over and over again. Blood poured from his scalp. ■ "You killed me," he screamed. "You killed me, woman. Don't hit me any more." ■ The baby was crying and Fernando was gushing blood all over the floor. I didn't know what had happened. Then I realized the baby was crying because we had been fighting. ■ I wrapped the baby in a blanket and took him out to the patio. I put him down on the ground, and lay down next to him. I felt alive. The sun was on my skin and I could feel the warm breath of my own baby. ■ Ana, the landlady came out and saw the machete. She asked if Don Fernando had been slaughtering chickens. "Where is he?" ■ "Who knows?" ■ Ana looked at the machete and smiled. "Look, Señora Alicia, as long as you have the chance, why not just go back to your mother? Fernando is going to kill you. Then what's going to become of your baby? Put some things together and leave them on the stairs. I'll pack them. Hurry up, you've got to leave before dusk. Fernando will be looking for his supper by then." ■ I packed a few things. Ana gave me twenty pesos and directions to the bus. I wasn't even sure if Mama would take me in.

I stayed at home for a year. I gave birth to my second baby alone in the house. Mama wouldn't help me. She said I could walk to the hospital, but it was too late. Miguelito tried to help, but he didn't know what to do. With two babies it was impossible to live in Mama's house. ■ One day I was killing time in the cafeteria — maybe I was out of work or maybe I'd had a fight at home with Javier and Mama. Ever since Javier found out I was pregnant with Daniel he'd been cruel to me. Anyway there was a newspaper in the cafeteria — there was a story in it about a new *invasión*. The picture showed people cowering behind trees, and the caption said the cops had no heart. ■ I kept thinking about it. Alirio, an old tenant, stopped by. He was living in the new settlement. (It was called Luis Alberto Vega after the man who was killed in the battle for Policarpa.) Mama said, "Why don't you go live there too?" ■ "Yes," Alirio said. "Get your things ready. I'll pick you up in a taxi at nine tomorrow morning." ■ Nine o'clock, no Alirio, no car. Ten o'clock, nothing. Noon, still nothing. There I was on the street with my kids and my bags. Finally, at four in the afternoon, we got a cab by ourselves. ■ We drove uphill past embassy row and the beautiful houses with big gardens — it didn't look like any new barrio was happening here — and we kept going through eucalyptus groves, till the car stopped where the road ended and all traces of the city faded away. ■ I took my sons Daniel and Hernando by the hand. I looked up at the mountain, then down on the city. "My God! What am I doing? I'm going to die here. And I've dreamed of so many things. Look at me — here I am burying my whole life." ■ I walked along with wet eyes and my mattress on my shoulder and my pots in my hand and I looked at the string of tiny black houses along the road. This was different from other *invasiones* because it was the forest. I was struck by how the trees were all green and the earth was brown but the houses were black — not like where I had grown up. ■ I thought about a day in December in Mama's first house in Bogotá, when I was a little girl, when Javier and I were sitting in the doorway watching Señora Reyes's guinea pigs and thinking about

Christmas and wondering if we would get any presents. It was hard to believe the baby Jesus played favorites, but it seemed to me that he was more generous to rich kids. ■ At school that year they were looking for a girl with very long hair to play the Virgin Mary on Christmas Eve and ride in one of those carts decorated with flowers. I knew my hair was long enough, but I was only seven. I wanted to ask the man if I could ride on the cart anyway, but Mama wouldn't let me leave the house. ■ Now I remembered how Mama had fought for a roof over her children's heads; she was the model I worked from. ■ The kids and I climbed the steps notched into the mountain to a field that was bald except for a single clump of eucalyptus trees. Other people were arriving with their belongings. I set down my mattress and put the pots under a bush. We picked up rocks and sticks and began to build our house. Friends began to stop by with coffee and greetings and twenty pesos, whatever they had. The kids were running around. We were making something for ourselves. ■ Three days later, when our shack was finished, the kids and I stood on the road below, gazing up at it. We looked at it to make sure it existed. ■ "You remember before?" I said to the kids. "When we didn't have a house, only this mattress in your grandma's room? Then you found sticks and bricks to make our new house strong. When you grow up, I want you to be independent. This shack is a lesson. When you're older, we'll have more things, better things. But it's good to build in stages."

The Monday after we arrived, people started getting evicted. The cops came, and the mayor; our lawyers from the housing group came and argued with the mayor and the cops about pieces of paper. We said show us the land titles, but there weren't any. ■ Somebody put the national anthem on a tape recorder. The cavalry rode in. The people from the barrio higher up the mountain scrambled down shouting and screaming. The cops tried to drag the women from their houses, but we formed a human chain and held on. "Don't leave," I yelled. "Don't leave. Even if they beat you, don't leave." A cop tore the clothes off one of the women. We chanted: "*Dónde está el pueblo? El pueblo dónde está? El pueblo está en las calles buscando unidad.*

Los barrios unidos jamás serán vencidos." ("Where are the people? The people, where are they? The people are getting together in the streets. United neighborhoods will never be conquered.") ■ The cops clubbed a woman with a little boy. When the boy saw his mother bleeding, he threw a rock at the cops and the cops busted his head. ■ Then the president of Luis Alberto Vega — she was a very elegant woman — asked the cops in a calm voice not to harm the people. And please not to go into their houses — that was a crime. They represented the law and they had to obey it. They must consider the children and old people. ■ Something about her voice must have embarrassed them, if such a thing is possible. They backed off for a while. The settlement spread. When new people came, we asked, "Where are you from, what do you want?" We made sure no spies got in. A lot of con artists showed up with lines like, "Why suffer in this dump?" They'd offer to rent you a room — anything to take over the land. ■ We patrolled the *invasión*, and in the early evening hours it was lovely work. Sometimes I did two watches a night. I put the children to sleep and then went out. They were fine. And I made a hundred pesos a shift. ■ If something went wrong, we clanged an iron bar hanging from a eucalyptus tree. If a man came home drunk and started beating up on his wife, somebody would ring the alarm and we'd grab the guy and teach him a lesson — tie him to a post and throw water on him. Once, when the city cops happened to be there, they joined in and dragged a wife beater behind one of their horses. ■ When I was a kid in Policarpa, there was this boy, Feliciano, a seminary student, who became a priest. You could tell he had something — a special strength and kindness. One day he showed up in Policarpa wearing street clothes, so we asked him, "Are priests supposed to dress that way?" ■ Feliciano was still a very shy boy; he smiled and blushed and said, "No, but let's just say I'm on vacation." ■ For a while he came to every one of our community meetings, then he disappeared. People said he was traveling. One afternoon the newspaper carried a huge picture of him on the front page. Father Feliciano had been executed by the army for being a guerrilla. "A guerrilla? But Feliciano was a priest," I said to Mama. ■ "Yes, dear, but he changed. He changed his religion for politics." ■ Politics aren't fair. So why should a poor person get

149

involved in politics? To get screwed? ■ I saw people kill each other for stupid ideologies, because they weren't educated. I saw politicians behaving like animals trying to make us believe they have something different to offer, while they're all eating from the same table. Politicians are one big family; they intermarry to perpetuate the dominant species. ■ Our strength doesn't come from politicians. Who gives us our daily bread? A politician? Sure, he might tell you, when a job opens up, he'll call you. So you leave a hundred pesos worth of application forms in an employment office instead of buying milk for your kids. So who should we have faith in? Living in Luis Alberto Vega, I began to develop my own ideas about what justice should be.

A year after we built our house, a general strike — the first ever — was announced. They were calling for a fifty percent raise in the workers' salaries, and better roads and services. I had to decide whether to participate or not. I was working at the airport, selling food. Prices had gone up but wages hadn't. We could barely afford to buy a piece of meat every other week. We were working harder and getting poorer all the time. So it was an easy decision, except for the kids. What would happen to them if I went to jail? Daniel was only two years old. I'd have to be very careful; I had to play the game as well as I could. The army was saying that all barrios like ours were war zones, so I knew that under martial law I could be arrested as a war criminal. ■ I put on blue jeans and a black jacket, which got a smile from Flavio, the organizer I'd met the night before at the committee meeting. (He only called himself Flavio; it was a code name he picked in honor of a great uncle of his. Mine was Sylvia, after a soap opera star.) We were supposed to pose as a married couple. ■ It was a normal day except there were more cops on the corners with shields and camouflage uniforms. The plan was, we'd go down into the city at night. The workers were going out on strike and it was our job to stop the trucks from bringing merchandise into the city. Flavio was wearing overalls so the cops would take him for a construction worker on the night shift. ■ At midday we walked down the mountain to Chapinero, which is a shopping center full of fancy clothes and food from all over the world. On Sixty-seventh Street there were cops with machine guns, some with bayonettes and shields. ■ We'd hidden a pile of scrap lumber in an empty lot on Sixty-fifth Street. The idea was to hammer nails in the boards and scatter them across Seventh Avenue, the main road leading out of Bogotá to the north. ■ Flavio spilled his nails. Six cops stood him against the wall of a fancy lingerie store, and started kicking him. One of them grabbed my purse, which I'd stuffed with romance novels to bury the nails I was carrying. ■ "And what do we have here?" asked a light-skinned officer who seemed to be in charge of the others. "Just a few love stories, sir." ■ "Don't you know there's a curfew?" The officer handed me back my bag. ■ I flung it against Flavio's stomach. "You miserable ungrateful son of a bitch — why did you make me leave the house? I've got so much washing to do. Now look where we are. I should've ditched you years ago." ■ Flavio grabbed my elbow. "Who the hell are you calling a son of a bitch, you bitch? I took you to the goddamn church, you think you own me." ■ "Both of you shut up and get in the van," the cop who'd taken my bag yelled. ■ "I told you we'd get in trouble, dick-head. Mama always said I married a clown who couldn't keep his zipper shut and she was right." ■ "You cunt!" Flavio slapped me across the face (but lightly, so my cheek burned for only a second). ■ A black cop with a Caribbean accent grabbed Flavio's wrists, twisted them behind his back, and shoved him in the van. "Now Madam Sylvia," he said, "would you please accompany your husband?" He goosed me and pushed me in. ■ The van was big and there was a screen that separated us from the cab. I thought about my kids asleep in the house by themselves. ■ "You really are a prick — you know that, Flavio? I could be home washing diapers. Who's going to clean the kids' shit while I'm in jail just because you want to go out and get drunk? No way, my friend! I've had it." ■ The black cop was driving and an officer with a white leather holster was sitting on the passenger side giving him directions. We headed south — to the station I thought. But we kept going farther and farther. Flavio and I kept arguing. The officer told us to shut up. Flavio lay his head back and shut his eyes, I imagined, to calm himself, and I sniffled, "Oh my God, oh my God...," and then I started doing my frustrated wife routine again, thinking about Fernando even though I hadn't seen him for two years. We kept it up for an hour. Then I didn't recognize the streets and buildings anymore. ■ "Let's get rid of these morons," the officer said. "I'm sick of listening to their crap. They're too stupid to be subversives." ■ They dropped us in front of what looked like a garbage dump. It was a barrio like ours, only it was full of rag pickers who collected garbage every day to sell. Three young sisters who were sorting metal from one of the piles showed us where to catch a bus back to the city. ■ It was very cold that evening and the wind had ripped off a piece of my roof. I put the kids to bed and piled coats and sweaters over them. ■ When we'd left Luis Alberto Vega that morning we'd arranged to meet the others at five o'clock at my house. By six no one had come. There was a seven o'clock curfew. Flavio said he had to look for our friends. ■ I put on a pair of loose pants and stuffed a pillow under one of my maternity blouses. When the kids fell asleep, I went to meet Flavio. I took a prescription the doctor had given me for Daniel. Flavio and I were walking down the mountain when a flashlight blinded us. The place was crawling with cops. ■ "Should we go?" Flavio asked me. I guess he thought I'd split as soon as I saw the cops. I stuck my stomach out as far as I could and staggered straight toward them. ■ They sounded like a chorus of a stupid song: "Halt! Don't you know there's a curfew? Halt! Don't you know you're risking your lives? Halt! Don't you know there's a curfew? Halt!" ■ I put my hand on my stomach and made a sick face. Flavio grabbed my waist to hold me up. "No, no, she's dying. We're going to the doctor." ■ I reached in my pocket and found the prescription. A tall cop shined his flashlight on it. The other cops passed the paper around, examining the address and the indecipherable prescription Dr. Quintana had written for Daniel's cough. I moaned and grabbed Flavio. ■ "Brothers," Flavio said. "Please let us go. She's dying." ■ "Get going!" the first cop said. "But to the doctor. If we see you here again, we'll lock you up." They all leaned on their gun barrels, gripping them just below the bayonets and aiming them at the sky. ■ For two hours Flavio and I walked around the neighborhood looking for our friends, staying in the shadows. The streets were empty. Flavio walked me around the police barricade near my house and then he left. We were supposed to separate as soon as we finished working and not speak to each other again. ■ The next morning, plainclothes cops were all over Luis Alberto Vega. Our friends had been picked up, taken to jail, and tortured. I went out to buy bread. "Alicia, how did it go last night?" my neighbor's kids called. I looked around to see if any cops were close. "Sssh, ssshhhh," I said. "Go inside and don't talk about last night anymore." ■ The others were in jail for months. They talked, so I couldn't risk leaving the barrio. I used my false name until we decided the danger had passed. Flavio got home all right, but he had to stop organizing until the others were released. ■ Forty people were killed, hundreds were wounded and over four thousand were arrested. But it worked. We shut down the city that day.

When we were living in El Valle, Grandfather Leónidas almost stopped planting coca because fewer and fewer people chewed it. The only people who still used it were the old folks and the kids whose parents gave it to them so they'd work harder. When they grew up, they felt ashamed, and stopped chewing it. ■ My godfather cultivated ten or fifteen coca plants by his house. He chewed coca to work; it gave him strength, he said. After breakfast, the workers picked a few leaves of coca and toasted them in a pan until they were tender. They let the coca cool and put it in a tray with a cloth on top, pressing it flat. Each man picked up his ration — as many leaves as would fit between his thumb and index finger — and stuck it in the little bag he carried. Later he mashed it with a stone and chewed and chewed and chewed until it got like chewing gum. Then the men went off to work in the fields. They said the coca made their heads hot. Then outsiders invaded the land to plant coca. When they began processing it in the village, everyone started growing it. My family got good money for it. Strange people came and went. Around dusk, somebody would pick up ten or twenty or thirty sacks of coca. Sometimes people came to weigh it and pack it on the donkeys. They took it just like that — green. I never knew where they processed it. ■ In 1978 we returned to El Valle and Mama made 45,000 pesos in seven months. The job went like this: Grandmother or one of my uncles told us that Señor So-and-So had ordered so many sacks of coca, so that's how many you had to pick that day. We delivered the sacks, they paid us. That was the whole story. When we went back five years later, everybody was talking about processing it themselves. And talking about *basuco* — something like what the foreigners call crack.

By the time Miguelito was seventeen, he was smoking a lot of *basuco*. He learned the stone mason's trade from Raúl — whom he stayed with sometimes. Then he went to Cartagena to hang marble veneer on the new hotels. He stayed almost a year. When he got back people hired him to build houses. ■

His buddy Nestor, who was studying to be a car mechanic, lived a half-block away. Nestor hired him as a helper, but he had a habit of getting Miguelito drunk and taking his money and rolling him down the stairs into the street. That friendship didn't last long. ■ Next thing, Miguelito's girlfriend Esmeralda started driving him crazy. She got pregnant by another guy. But they kept seeing each other. Esmeralda promised that after the kid was born she'd stop going out with other guys. Everybody said, how is he going to support her and the kid? Then her mother happened to mention to Miguelito that Esmeralda was married to Roberto the shoemaker. That's when Miguelito started smoking marijuana and then *basuco*. ■ He was a sweet guy, but now he was coming home stoned and calling Mama a whore. He smashed the walls with a sledgehammer, then he went after Mama. She called the cops and they told him if he didn't behave they'd fine him 5,000 pesos or lock him up. "I'm going to build myself a room right here in Mama's house," he said. But he didn't, he left. ■ Miguelito landed in the jungle building swimming pools for the "tourists" (as they called themselves): the drug Mafia, who paid him in coca. Nobody lived in the jungle except the Mafia, and who knows what it's like since the army moved in and bulldozed their private airports and burned everything down? Miguelito ran away to El Valle. My uncle was growing coca there, so he hired Miguelito at two sacks a week. A cousin brought him back to Bogotá. His hair was cut short, he'd filled out, and he was quiet. ■ When Miguelito was a little boy he wanted to be a detective, because guns were the most mysterious things he could think of, so he volunteered for the army with the idea of being close to guns, getting off drugs and maybe going to the jungle. ■ The recruits were separated into two lines, one for the jungle, the other for Bogotá. Miguelito slipped out of the city line and cut into the jungle one. So he went to the jungle plains of Meta, but his papers stayed in Bogotá. ■ His real trouble started at the induction ceremony where they gave out the guns. There were hundreds of boys. The general called each one and handed him a rifle. A helicopter landed, the general walked off, and the first lieutenant took over. ■ The helicopter took off right away. Miguelito heard some swearing and he saw the general, but then the general disappeared. Another helicopter landed. Very slowly, Miguelito walked closer. Soldiers were carrying huge sacks. He reached into one and felt something like powdered milk in nylon bags. He licked his fingers. It tasted sharp; it was cocaine. He started helping the soldiers load the helicopters. The first helicopter took off; then the second helicopter took off. The general who'd been handing out guns appeared and asked Miguelito what he was doing. ■ "They ordered me to help load, sir." ■ "Keep your stupid nose out of this. Go stand with the recruits." ■ But Miguelito wanted to see where the sacks were going, so he hid behind some crates till the general left. The first helicopter landed again. Again he helped load sacks. He counted the sacks that were left and figured the next trip would be the last. When no one was looking, he started to climb the helicopter stairs, but the second his foot touched the stair he was hit from behind. He turned but nobody was there. He sat down on the tarmac, convinced that something superhuman had knocked him off the stairs. ■ Suddenly he was surrounded. Where did he live? Was he a member of the M-19, the revolutionary movement that was popular in the cities? Was he a communist, a guerrilla? ■ "No, no," he said; he lived in Policarpa. ■ "Well, that's a communist barrio. And you're a communist." ■ "No, no, I'm not a communist." ■ They gave him permission to call home, but Miguelito couldn't get through. In Luis Alberto Vega there was only one public phone — whoever answered it announced the message over the loudspeaker, "Señora Alicia Vásquez to the telephone." When Miguelito put the phone down, the officer who had given him the phone-pass offered him a soda. He drank it and passed out and woke up in the barracks. ■ They ripped off his uniform and dragged him naked, feet first, to show him off to the other recruits. They stood him up in the compound, then knocked him down and kicked him in the head. They doused him with ice water and dragged him back to the cell. When he came to, he was still naked and every bone in his body felt broken. His street clothes were in the corner. He got dressed and pounded on the door. And pounded and pounded. He passed out again and this time he woke up in solitary. ■ Finally one of the guards let him call again. Miguelito told me where he was and we talked for fifteen minutes. The next day they let him walk around for an hour. A few days later I came to see him. They said wait, he's doing laundry. But when I saw his dirty hands, I knew they were lying. Miguelito said he was feeling fine, just fine. One of his buddies took me aside and said, "Look, you better take your brother home soon or they're going to kill him." ■ For six weeks he stayed in the cell, a narrow dark room with no toilet. They shoved bread and water under the door. Sometimes only water. Miguelito sent word through his buddy, who was getting released. The boy said, "Look, you better send money and clothes; they stopped feeding him." But Miguelito got out before I could do this. The conductor gave him a free ride to Bogotá. He came home filthy and barefoot. They'd discharged him on the grounds that he had a drug problem. ■ He got a job working for a cabinet maker who'd been kind enough to hire him even though he was a mess. One day it rained so hard the workshop flooded. The next day Miguelito came to work completely stoned and fell face down in the mud. The cabinet maker said he couldn't keep him, he was making his customers nervous. He paid him a day's pay. Miguelito went outside and sat in the puddles. ■ He smoked *basuco* in the bathroom of Mama's house. He bought it outside the hospital from a dealer named Little Cat, who eventually got machine-gunned by the cops. Two or three times a week, whenever the cops picked him up, he'd call me. "I'm in the station at San Cristóbal," he'd say, or wherever. "They picked me up last night and they'll let me out tomorrow." Sometimes he called frightened: "Come and get me or I'm joining the guerrillas; I'm not going to jail." ■ One night he didn't come home. I got frantic. I looked for him in the hospitals, in the police stations, in the morgues. That was the last time he called. He'd stolen our boarder's stereo. Mama reported him, her own son. ■ They gave him five days in the stockade, no food, then they transferred him to the Modelo prison. He lived off scraps the other prisoners gave him. (Nobody told us we were supposed to bring him a blanket and dishes and food.) When he tried to stand up, his legs folded. But even when there wasn't food, there were drugs. The guards used to make all visitors strip and do deep knee bends so they could see if you were carrying anything in your vagina or up your ass, and women weren't allowed to go in with high heels and you had to leave your shoelaces and belt with the guards. Bringing in dope was the guards' exclusive business. ■ Miguelito's mind went. He started talking and laughing to himself and jerking his head like a chicken. They confiscated his shoes and released him. He hung around Luis Alberto Vega for a while. Then he disappeared. ■ I never saw Miguelito again, but my uncles in El Valle say he was there with a buddy. I don't know if it was just meanness in the family but my uncle said he saw Miguelito's body at the bottom of a canyon. Then there was a rumor that the guerrillas had executed him but that doesn't make sense to me. They execute their enemies in public, so everyone will know. Maybe it was the army, or just drugs, or maybe he's still alive. Who knows? He was such a beautiful boy.

The communists say that a person is a material thing and there is no infinite power. There is no God, the communists say; a human being is the same as a plant you sow in the ground. If you cultivate it, it grows, reproduces, and dies. It doesn't have a spirit or a soul. A person is alive because his blood is pumping through his body. When he dies, the blood stops. I've seen too many things to believe that. ■ On my Uncle Luis's farm there were *duendes* — wind spirits. They were small boys with large green hats who came out in the late afternoon. They took the professor's son into the mountains. When he wandered home two days later, the skin on his face had peeled off and his clothes were in pieces. He said the boys with green hats had led him by the hand deep under the earth. ■ The old people used to be terrible. Their way was to lay a curse on anyone they got mad at. One time somebody put a spell on my Grandmother Pepita, and Don Arturo, the healer, pulled a long piece of straw from one of her ears and a grain of corn from the other. ■ "Your sons will be thieves and your daughter will belong to the street," my grandmother told Mama. Well, I haven't become a streetwalker, but my brothers. . . they've hit Mama with their own hands. ■ When Grandfather left for work, Grandmother made Mama work harder than anyone else. "You're very proud, María," she said. "You're like your father, you think you're better than the rest of us. People like us, María, we're born to serve." ■ When my grandmother was pregnant with my youngest aunt, Mama brought her a piece of cheese in bed. ■ "Put it on the table, María; I'm not in any shape to eat cheese. Your father just gave me some medicine. Are you going to the party?" ■ There was a party that night for Grandfather's godchild. He said Mama could go. By ten o'clock the musicians were drunk, so they left. When they got home, Grandmother had already had the baby. ■ "Did you dance a lot?" she asked. ■ "Yes, but the party finished early." ■ "You little black bitch! I was sick, you were dancing. The day you have your first child, worms will crawl out from your womb. Then you'll realize you shouldn't have left your mother alone." She started to cry. "Because you didn't have the courtesy to get me even a glass of water, you will suffer for five days and five nights just as I did with my first child." ■ When Mama got pregnant she thought about Grandmother's curse. They were in the tropics and it was a hot summer. Papa tried to take care of her, but she suffered just like Grandmother said. ■ Javier was born at five in the morning. Papa cut the cord, Mama dressed the baby in new clothes, and then she passed out. She woke up at midnight and there were lots of people scurrying around the bed. They said she'd died. Papa was crying. Mama was swollen. They gave her medicine. She said she felt her insides explode and she vomited. The placenta came out and she started hemorraging. Papa fed her with his own hands and carried her from one bed to another. He did love her. ■ She said she hurt so much she couldn't straighten up for three days. Her vagina began to burn and itch and she felt something buzzing beneath the covers. She stopped bleeding hard but she noticed yellow water with the blood. She asked Papa to look. "How could your mother be so cruel?" he shouted.

Grandfather used to work with a man named Manuel Medina who played the guitar and had a very beautiful wife named Judith. This Judith made up her mind that when she reached thirty she'd kill herself because she didn't want to get old and ugly; she didn't want people to see her all full of wrinkles. On her thirtieth birthday her friends gave her presents, which made her very happy. Then, that same night, she fired a bullet into her head. But her friends took her to the hospital and she didn't die. ■ Three months later she drank poison but she still didn't die. Then she threw herself off the bridge. She didn't die that time either, because a gust of wind blew her onto a pile of bamboo branches. She just lay there tangled up till somebody found her. ■ On her thirty-fifth birthday, she spent a wild night with her friends, got smashed on *aguardiente*. Then she went home and blasted herself with a fancy revolver she'd bought. That time she died. ■ Grandfather was the casket maker for the village. He came and lifted Judith out of bed, laid her out on a straw mat and covered her with a sheet. He cut four banana branches, made holes in them, set candles by the body and built the coffin. The women took her clothes off and washed her. They trimmed her fingernails. ■ They dressed Judith in a black cap and black dress she'd had made for her thirtieth birthday. They tied a rope around her waist. I remember when my great-grandmother died, Grandfather bought a piece of black cloth with tiny stars on it so Mama could make her burial dress. Judith hadn't planned for this, so there was only time now to use her birthday dress, and a mantle for her head. Underneath, the women always wore a white skirt and black stockings — no shoes. They made the stockings out of the same material they made the shroud from. And if the corpse was very poor and couldn't afford stockings, they cleaned the feet and left them barefoot. ■ They put Judith in Grandfather's casket and arranged the candles around it. Next day they buried her. For nine nights her friends sang hymns.

Once there was a young girl whose mother wanted her to marry a rich man much older than she was. She didn't like him, so she left home for El Valle. The rich man sent a posse to find her. He married her, but she refused to live with him. His pride was so hurt he sent for a witch to cast a spell on her, to keep her from ever sleeping with a man. ■ Her body balled up in the fetal position. She couldn't stretch her limbs. Her mother had to carry her everywhere. The rich man found another woman, built a house, and had children. When he died the poor woman was still living all drawn up. ■ Eighteen years later her mother brought her to Don Arturo. Don Arturo asked everyone who had a colt to keep the first cutting from its mane and bring it to him, so that he could braid it into a rope. He hung the rope from the roof and asked the girl to grab it. He hoisted her up. While she was hanging there, he fed her beans with three live fleas in them. The next day she was able to stretch her legs and walk. She said it was like she had just been born.

Ever since I was a little girl, I've been ambitious. I wanted to learn things, I wanted to get off the road poor people keep walking on. I didn't just want to have kids and beat them the way Mama did. How many mothers wish their children had a place where no one could make fun of them, where no one could mistreat them? ■ After we finished building our shacks, some of the women in Luis Alberto Vega got together and formed a cooperative to make handicrafts. Every afternoon the women came to my house and sewed patchwork scenes of the barrio, of our everyday lives. We made lamps out of glass bottles we'd scavenged. I brought the cloth pictures and the lamps to the handicraft stores in Bogotá. Sometimes the church workers, who had helped us start up the cooperative, sent them to America to sell. ■ Everything changed for me when I started this project. Life wasn't just the same old thing; I was doing something for the other women. When we worked together, we talked about our problems and how we could solve them. ■ Some of the women complain. "Ay, Señora Alicia, my husband won't give me any money for the market. . . . My husband is seeing another woman. . . . My husband beats me up. . . ." ■ Adam and Eve were equal. Ever since then, it's been a battle. When the complaining starts, I say to myself, "What do I have to whine about? I don't have a man to bother me." ■ When I left Fernando, people said, "Alicia, you're a bad one. You're too proud. You shouldn't humiliate a man. Don't do that." ■ Maybe I am vain, but it wasn't vanity to see that Fernando wasn't providing a good home for the children and me. The way I think about things has changed since we built the shack. I've become a planner. I keep an inventory of each day. ■ Maybe the things I plan are illusions, but I see progress all around me, in places I least expect it. I see it in the way the kids today are more aware than we were. They speak up for themselves. My generation was taught to keep our mouths shut. I tell my kids, "When you see me doing something wrong, tell me — I'm only human." They tell me, all right. ■ I can give my sons many things from my own life, but I don't want them to get stranded in the middle of the road. So I make sure they go to school every day and I ask them to show me what they're learning. It's sad to see a kid lugging potatoes to market or collecting garbage the way my brother did. ■ The changes have been slow, but they come at my pace. My eyes are okay now. If I find myself looking enviously at someone, something inside tells me to back off. What gives me the most pleasure is knowing I can hold my own kids in my arms and knowing my eyes won't hurt them. ■ When I get to feeling down and I don't think I'll be able to take care of the kids and myself, I say, "I've got to do it and I can do it." Grandfather Marco Tulio had the same power. Where did it come from? ■ Marco Tulio built our house with adobe bricks when he was young; it looked like it sprang up through the dirt. There were round clay pots on the wood fire to cook the rice and soup. There was a pile of eucalyptus branches on the floor next to the stove made of piled stones. The space above the stove was dark. The roof was bamboo blackened by thirty years of cooking smoke.

In my dreams I still walk the coffee fields looking for Papa and my grandparents. I still see the dawn clouds hanging so low over the valley, hiding the mountains. It's always cold and quiet. When the mist is thick, I open and close the door quickly because I'm afraid the clouds might come in and cover up Mama and Papa and Javier. On Volcano Ridge, I see the chickens and goats and sheep lining up in front of my grandfather's house, cackling and bleating, waiting to be fed. ❧ I lay my head on the ground next to the chicks at feeding time, so they'll mistake my teeth for kernels of corn and peck at them. I kiss their tiny sharp beaks; they feel like needles. I grow a beak and peck them back. When I play with the sheep, I have horns and fur. After Mama and Papa slaughter Apple, my goat, I tie his horns with a leather strap and wear them around my forehead. ❧ There is one big room where Mama cooks and we all sleep with Papa's brother and two sisters, Ana Julia and Mercedes. The girls' bed is a wooden platform along the wall underneath the window. Mercedes kicks off the covers. She makes a fuss about the corn borers that keep dropping from the ceiling and crawling all over her legs and toes. "The bed is eating me," she says. ❧ Ana Julia has just turned fourteen and I like to look at her new body. Her shirt is torn down the front, so I can see her small breasts poking through. When she washes clothes in the river, I go with her. She kneels on the bank and arches her back and thumps the soapy clothes on a flat rock and her breasts bounce through her cotton blouse. I stick my hand underneath to feel them and she calls me a naughty little devil.

Now I have a long white nightgown. Sometimes at night I get the urge to go out and look at the mountains and the city or the sky — it's so beautiful when it's clear. These nights, the old men and women in the barrio swear they see a witch in a long white gown walking through the eucalyptus.

END ■■■

■ LIST OF PHOTOGRAPHS ■■■■■■■■■■■■■■■■■■■■■■■■

The photographs in this book, listed by page number below, were taken by Wendy Ewald throughout Colombia with a two and a quarter format camera from 1982 to 1988 and by her fifth grade students in Ráquira, Colombia with Instamatic cameras in 1982 and 1983.

■ NOTES ON THE PHOTOGRAPHS ■■■■■■■■■■■■■■■■■■■
■■■■■■■■■■■ BY THE CHILDREN OF RÁQUIRA, COLOMBIA

■ Some people worry that I'll use a picture of them to cast a spell. We all believe that, in one way or another. I've heard it said that you should never give a photograph of yourself away. ■ I like to take photographs of my family so their memories will remain after they die. In twenty years when I look at the photographs I might think: "Oh! what a different life that was. What a hard time I had." ■ I'm proud to know how to pick up the camera and take pictures. The gringo tourists always come to take pictures of us when we're making pots. When I was small I was excited by it. I never thought about why they were doing it. Now I'm ashamed to think I might look funny or distracted in pictures that might end up in a newspaper or a movie. ■ I teach my brothers and sisters and the other kids how to use the camera. But sometimes the older kids see me with the camera and they say, "Hey, you don't know how to take pictures." So I have to take their picture and give it to them to prove it. Who knows? One day I could be a professional. ■ I get very excited when I approach people to take their pictures. Sometimes it's delicate because they start to ask questions. What do I get out of it? When they respond that way I feel ashamed and cheated because I value those people. ■ I like to wait to take my pictures when people are doing something special, like dancing, working or at Christmas. I wait for the right moment. . . but sometimes I arrange things so that a mop or something untidy isn't in the picture, or I ask someone not to pass through. ■ Sometimes I wait and wait and nothing happens. Then I make up a photograph. There are so many things (like my family, the beautiful animals we have, the inside of the house and what goes on) to take pictures of that I don't know what to take. I keep my photographs in the cracker box and when I don't have anything to do I look at the best ones. ■ I'm glad that you people outside our village can see these photographs because you'll learn a lot about us. ■ Don't praise us; we're nothing special, just ordinary country children, but we're grateful.